D1206235

THE FUTURE OF NATIONALIZATION

The Future of Nationalization

BY

H. A. CLEGG
Fellow of Nuffield College, Oxford

AND

T. E. CHESTER
of the Acton Society Trust

BASIL BLACKWELL
OXFORD
1953

Printed in Great Britain for Basil Blackwell & Mott, Limited
by A. R. Mowbray & Co. Limited in the City of Oxford

PREFACE

SINCE this essay was sent to the press the Conservative Government has presented two drafts of its Transport Bill to the House of Commons. These have, to some extent, revised the proposals of its White Paper on Transport Policy of May, 1952, which is discussed on p. 199. We have thought it inadvisable to change the text, both because the Bill may be amended further, and because the alterations made so far have not caused us to revise our opinions. If the Bill becomes law there will be an opportunity to recast railway organization. The decision to disband the Railway Executive could be a step in the right direction; but there is little reason to suppose that the Executive will not be succeeded by systems of regional organization closely akin to those of the four Main Line companies before nationalization. If reorganization is not taken further down to local organization within the railways, little will be done to remedy those shortcomings which had existed before nationalization and have persisted under nationalization.

There have been changes in the organization of other nationalized industries, for instance in the two Airways Corporations, and changes in the composition of the boards. The Ridley Committee has reported on fuel and power policy (Cmd. 8647 of 1952). For the reasons already mentioned we have not incorporated any reference to these events in the text.

We wish to record our gratitude to those who have read drafts of this essay and assisted us with their advice and suggestions. Amongst these we may name D. N. Chester, Fellow of Nuffield College, Oxford, and J. H. Smith, Assistant Lecturer in the Department of Social Administration at the London School of Economics (formerly of the Acton Society Trust). Others wish to remain anonymous. We would like also to express our thanks to the institutions in which we work—Nuffield College and the Acton Society Trust; in particular we are indebted to the Trustees of the Acton Society Trust for permission to use certain material incorporated in the essay. No one but ourselves, however, bears responsibility for the errors which remain in what we have written, or for the opinions we have expressed.

H. A. Clegg
T. E. Chester

December, 1952

CONTENTS

CHAP. PAGE

Preface v

I. Why Nationalization? 1

1. The Doctrinaire Approach . . . 3
   (*a*) The Socialists 3
   (*b*) The Trade Unions 7
   (*c*) The Ideology of Bigness . . 15

2. The Pragmatic Approach . . . 20
   (*a*) Coal 21
   (*b*) Electricity 25
   (*c*) Gas 28
   (*d*) Transport 31
   (*e*) Air Transport 36
   (*f*) Steel 37

3. The Public Corporation 40

II. The Organization of Nationalized Industry 48

1. Coal 50
   (*a*) The Growth of Organization . 50
   (*b*) Changes in Organization . . 59
   (*c*) Problems for the Future . . 63

2. Electricity 69
   (*a*) The Growth of Organization . 69
   (*b*) Problems of Organization . . 77

CHAP. PAGE

II.—*continued*

3. Gas 82
4. Fuel and Power Co-ordination . . 90
5. Transport 91
   (*a*) The British Transport Commission 91
   (*b*) The Hotels Executive . . 95
   (*c*) The Road Passenger Executive . 96
   (*d*) The Docks and Inland Waterways Executive 99
   (*e*) The London Transport Executive 101
   (*f*) The Road Haulage Executive . 105
   (*g*) The Railway Executive . . 108
   (*h*) Progress towards Transport Co-ordination 119
6. Civil Air Transport 123
7. Steel 129

III. An Analysis of Problems of Organization 131

1. Clearing the Ground . . . 131
2. The Size of Unit 136
3. The National Authority . . . 141
4. Departments and Specialist Services . 147
5. Industrial Relations . . . 153
6. Centralization and Decentralization . 158

IV. The Reorganization of Nationalized Industry 165

1. Some Disclaimers 165

CHAP. PAGE

IV.—*continued*

2. Coal 168
3. Electricity 179
4. Gas 182
5. The Co-ordination of Fuel and Power 184
6. The Transport Commission . . 185
7. The Railway Executive . . . 188
8. The Road Haulage Executive . . 197
9. Other Nationalized Industries . . 200
10. Finding the Managers . . . 201
11. Conclusion 206

THE FUTURE OF NATIONALIZATION

CHAPTER I

WHY NATIONALIZATION?

THE purpose of this essay is to describe the forms of organization developed by the industries nationalized since 1945, and to offer some comments upon them. Both these tasks require some introduction. For much of the organization can only be made intelligible by reference to discussions, writings, and reports which preceded the nationalization Acts, or to previous nationalization measures; and criticism can be sensible only if the intention of the nationalizers, the objects which the organizations were designed to achieve, are first set out.

Nationalization has been discussed for more than half a century, and during several periods before 1945 it became a matter of general controversy. The material for this introductory chapter is, therefore, embarrassing in its fullness. Hundreds of books and unnumbered pamphlets and articles have been written about nationalization. Parliament provides some nationalization Acts, rejected nationalization Bills, and very many pages of Hansard. With this go the evidence and reports of several Royal Commissions, and the reports of a number of Departmental Committees.

Conference Reports of political parties, especially the Labour Party, record debates on the subject, and the delegates to the Trades Union Congress have not left their views unexpressed.

To do justice to this material would require a large volume, and a volume of interest only to specialists. The bold aim of this chapter is to select the most significant elements from this material, and to systematize them so as to be readily comprehensible, without more distortion than is inevitably entailed by selection and fitting together. It is not our intention that this chapter should serve as a detailed study of the growth of British thought on nationalization. In it we are not attempting to put forward our own views, and we do not wish to justify nationalization or to attack it. Our aim is only to provide 'potted' information essential to sensible discussion of the forms of nationalization as they exist to-day. For this purpose we try to distinguish two approaches to nationalization—the doctrinaire approach and the pragmatic approach. The 'doctrinaires' include those who have talked and written in a general manner of what could be achieved by transferring industry to national ownership. The 'pragmatists' are those who have wanted to achieve a particular change in a particular industry, for instance, rationalization of electricity distribution, and have seen in national ownership a useful means of setting up an authority with the power to make the change. This distinction is admittedly arbitrary—many, perhaps most, supporters of nationalization proposals have made use of both kinds of argument—but it assists our exposition, and allows several important points to be emphasized.

1. The Doctrinaire Approach

(a) *The Socialists*

The words 'socialist' and 'socialism' have always covered a wide range of opinion and belief, and to-day they have ceased to have much meaning. Many would find it very difficult to answer the question, 'Are you a socialist?' unless it is understood to be the equivalent of 'Are you a member of the Labour Party?' or 'Do you vote Labour?' To what would one be committed by an answer 'Yes' or 'No'? Answers would probably be qualified: 'Yes, but . . .' or 'No, but . . .' Even if socialism was identified with belief in nationalization, it would not remove the difficulty, for both before and after the Labour Party in 1918 wrote 'the common ownership of the means of production' into the Party Objects detailed in its constitution it has included men and women with a great variety of views on nationalization.

It is possible, however, to identify a main stream in the conflicting currents of British socialist thought. The early socialist leaders and groups, for instance, Hyndman and his Social Democratic Federation, and the Webbs and their Fabian Society, had many serious differences, but they were close enough together on the subject of public ownership. Both groups were eclipsed by the Independent Labour Party which provided what socialism there was in the early Labour Party, and whose leaders—MacDonald, Snowden, Jowett, Lansbury—appeared before the country as 'the socialists.' During the difficult years of the 'twenties, when the I.L.P. drew away from the Labour Party, and when the first appearance of Soviet Russia and the

Communists, the General Strike and the poor showing of two Labour Governments caused differences to rankle and fester, no dominant trend is discernible; but during the 'thirties it can perhaps be seen in the revived Fabian Society and its writers—particularly a considerable group of University teachers of economics and other subjects who were associated with the Society.

The first concern of socialists has been with poverty and the evils which they attribute to it. Many besides socialists have been moved to try to remedy poverty, but the socialists are marked out by their belief that the public authorities should take on the responsibility, not only by organizing what are now called social services, but also by controlling production (to ensure that sufficient is produced to avoid poverty) and the distribution of incomes (to see that poverty does not arise from gross inequality). Their confidence that these means should give the results they desired is strengthened by their belief that enormous waste can be avoided only if production is carried on 'for use'; that is, if the productive and service industries are planned to produce what the public authorities decide is most necessary, and not left to make money as best they can.

The application of this doctrine to public ownership is not difficult. Socialists sought power to win their objectives, and this involved two stages: they had to get themselves elected in sufficient numbers on to public authorities; and they had to increase the powers of those public authorities to allow them scope to plan and control industry. Any extension of public ownership was thus a step in the right direction, and the early Fabians for a time concentrated their attention on 'gas and water' socialism. This, however, did not bring rapid results. A few progressive local authorities, for instance, could do little more than attempt to alleviate the worst cases of hardship. But if Parliament could be persuaded to act, to take over industry in large sections, socialism would come apace. Administratively this would mean taking over each industry as a separate monopoly—a process with which governments were already familiar, in this country with telegraphs and later with telephones, and in some foreign countries also with railways, tobacco, and other services and products.

Nationalization thus became a central feature in the socialist programme, and it was nationalization rather than public ownership. For public ownership includes ownership by local authorities. Industries, when taken over, would have to be subject to the authority of the national government, at least in their major decisions. The profit motive was wrong, and a nationalized industry should make no profit; any surplus should go to the nation, and the nation meant the Exchequer. At first the easiest means of achieving these objects seemed to be to transfer the industry to a government department on Post Office lines. The workers in the industry would, of course, benefit. The excision of profits would allow higher wages and better conditions, and they would know that they were not working to enrich the capitalist class. But the main beneficiary was to be the nation. The Fabians added a note of their own. The administration of industry was to be made far more efficient. The 'best brains' of the country were to manage industrial affairs. Promotion by merit was to replace nepotism. Statistics would be collected to allow decisions to be taken in full knowledge of the facts. The whole administrative machinery would be rationalized and streamlined, and would run smoothly and effectively.

Time and a changing environment affected socialist thought. After the first world war experience of government controls, the Russian Revolution, socialist governments in office, and Britain's chronic unemployment problem made 'Socialism in Our Time' seem a more practical and an ever more urgent aim. Nationalization must be supplemented by other measures which could give quick and marked results. Private industry was already subject to a number of controls—factory Acts, restrictions on hours, minimum wage legislation. The war showed that controls could be used far more widely than had seemed possible in the nineteenth century, by price restrictions, allocations, and the like. These means must be put to the service of socialism. Support came from the economists, some of whom found a socialist weapon in the Keynesian analysis, and argued that fiscal controls and redistribution of incomes could end unemployment.

At the same time expectations from nationalization were sobered down. Few would have cared to repeat the words of Hyndman—'When, as is the case to-day, two or three hours of labour out of the twenty-four by all adult males would be enough to give the whole community all the wholesome necessaries and comforts of life . . .'[1]—although such extravagances were common amongst early socialists. Now that nationalization Bills might find their way to the statute book, socialists

[1] *Socialism and Slavery*. H. M. Hyndman. The Modern Press, 1884. p. 17.

would rather say with Snowden: 'The advantages of nationalization would not be immediately obvious for it would take some time to get the new organization into successful working order,'[1] and talk of the need for the rehabilitation of industries which a decadent capitalism had allowed to become derelict.

So nationalization lost its pre-eminent position in the immediate socialist programme. Only for a few selected industries was it the next step. Public ownership, however, remained the ultimate goal, and nationalization the means to it. For when all was said in favour of other methods, control of industries owned and managed by capitalists, who might unwillingly obey, but were not likely to co-operate with zest, was a poor substitute for the direction of nationally-owned industries, managed by the best brains in the country, to fit in with a master plan for the whole economy.

(*b*) *The Trade Unions*

We do well to remind ourselves that in the early years of the Labour Party most of its trade union supporters were by no means socialists. They were trade unionists who wanted certain measures from Parliament to supplement their direct industrial work, and had been converted to the idea that they were more likely to get what they wanted from Parliament through a separate Labour Party than through hanging on to the 'Lib-Lab' coat-tails of the Liberal Party. Some trade unions, it must be admitted, notably of miners and railway workers, were won over to support for the nationalization of their own industries, but the

[1] *If Labour Rules.* Philip Snowden. Labour Publishing Co., 1923. p. 39.

main contribution of the unions to the theory of nationalization during those years was a heresy, a subversion both of official socialist doctrine and of official trade union doctrine, the heresy of industrial democracy; and amongst the heretics there were soon as many different opinions—syndicalism, industrial unionism, workers' control, guild socialism—as amongst the socialists themselves.

The main outlines of the doctrine are straightforward enough. Political socialism was attacked because it was failing to win big enough gains through parliamentary action, and because its projects of nationalization would only free the worker from bondage to the private capitalist in order to subject him to the state bureaucrat. Political action should be replaced by direct industrial action by which the workers should win power for themselves and then take over industry directly to be run for the benefit of the workers by their own organizations, the trade unions, reorganized into streamlined industrial unions for that purpose. Originally, the movement owed a good deal to inspiration from abroad, from the Syndicalists of France and the Industrial Workers of the World in the U.S.A., but during the first world war it developed its own indigenous forms. The shop stewards' movement, which for a time almost usurped the authority of the official trade union leaders over large areas of British industry, provided itself with an ultimate objective of 'workers' control' which owed much to the teaching of the small Socialist Labour Party, with its roots on the Clyde, to which many of its leaders belonged. At the same time a much more sophisticated political philosophy was developed by the Guild Socialists, whose main propagandist, G. D. H. Cole, was, as a wartime official of the Amalgamated Society of Engineers (now the Amalgamated Engineering Union), the ideal man to bridge the gap between the intellectuals and the rank and file activists. The Guild Socialists thought that public ownership might have to come through the action of the state, but that nationalized industries should be run by new organizations of 'workers by hand and brain' within each industry—the National Guilds—and the socialist society should be a partnership between the state, representing the whole body of citizens, particularly in their capacity of consumers, and the National Guilds representing the producers, brought together for certain purposes into a kind of general Industrial Parliament of Guilds.

The outcome of these developments was that at the end of the war there were a number of competent intellectuals ready to rewrite the Labour Party's nationalization proposals, and a large volume of support throughout the Labour movement from men and women influenced by often vague sentiment in favour of more industrial democracy and prepared to throw their weight behind any measure for 'workers' control.' When the Labour Party officially sponsored Bills for nationalization of the mines and later of the railways which were drawn up to carry out the principle of 'joint control' (management by a board partly of state nominees and partly of trade union delegates), the new movement seemed to have gained a great victory. It was, however, only a tactical retreat on the part of the orthodox socialists. The movement for 'workers' control' crumbled under the blows of the depression of 1921, 'Black Friday' (when the 'Triple Alliance,' of transport workers, railwaymen, and miners, broke down) and the subsequent Miners' Lock-out. The remnants were swept away by the General Strike of 1926. The Guild Socialists, as such, disappeared. All that was left was a vague feeling that nationalization should give workers a greater say in industry, and a positive demand that at least one member of the board of any public corporation should be drawn from the trade unions.

Not all political socialists would have gone so far as Snowden in saying:

'The difficulty of a Labour Administration in conducting national enterprises will more likely be at the bottom than at the top. This was the experience of Labour Governments in Australia with their nationalization undertakings. At first there was a disposition on the part of some of the workmen to bring pressure upon the Labour Government by their votes to grant unreasonable concessions.'[1]

Most of them were, however, prepared to go a long way with Herbert Morrison when he returned to the Fabian doctrine of the 'best brains' in his battle over the London Passenger Transport Bill during the second Labour Government, and argued that members of public boards should be chosen solely for their talent and experience, and should represent no interest. Trade union leaders also came to accept much of Morrison's point of view concerning nationalization—by a devious route. The 'Mond-Turner' talks (between the General Council of the T.U.C. and a group of 'progressive' employers brought together by Sir Alfred

[1] Op. cit., p. 28.

Mond), which followed the General Strike, were anti-socialist in the sense that they were an attempt by trade unions to obtain their objects through collaboration with private employers, but they revealed a consciousness on the part of the leaders that traditional trade union action was not enough. The intractable unemployment problem, coupled with a fairly steady and heart-breaking decline in trade union membership from the 1920 peak, forced home the point that collective bargaining can only be successful in a favourable environment. To produce that environment unions were prepared to collaborate with capitalists.

The 'Mond-Turner' talks were fruitless, and the economic difficulties of the 'twenties were followed by the disastrous depression of the early 'thirties. Since both collective bargaining and collaboration had proved insufficient, political action was now the only weapon, and trade union leaders, many perhaps for the first time, became convinced nationalizers. If this was the outcome of a capitalist economy, capitalism must go.

The benefits which union leaders expected to obtain, first from collaboration and then from nationalization, were increased employment, greater industrial efficiency, and consequent wage increases. They wanted to control the banks (to which they attributed the financial panic of 1931), to control investment, and to make big decisions affecting whole industries. Accordingly, they laid themselves open to most of the criticisms which the industrial democrats had made against an earlier generation of socialists; but no rank and file movement arose to attack their 'bureaucratic' methods. For workers themselves were far more interested in finding or keeping a job than in the control of decisions affecting their job by a workshop democracy.

Consequently, although Morrison's 'expert' board was hotly criticized at several Trade Union Congresses for its omission of direct trade union representation, it was ultimately accepted. Trade unions were certainly interested in the position they would hold under nationalization, but, in practice, their leaders showed themselves more concerned to ensure that public enterprise should accept the established pattern of industrial relations, should work through the normal machinery of collective bargaining and recognize the appropriate unions as the proper representatives of the workers for this purpose, than to carry out the demands of a movement which had grown up, at least in part, as a challenge to their own authority, and a movement which they no longer even feared.

Despite the collapse of their movement, the industrial democrats did leave their mark on the nationalization programme. The sections on public ownership in the 1944 Interim Report on Post-War Reconstruction of the T.U.C. General Council are perhaps most noteworthy on the grounds that they constituted a clear repudiation of the doctrine of 'workers' control' by the trade union leaders on the eve of the nationalization measures of the first Labour Government. But the report also claimed that:

'The Trade Union Movement exists to extend the influence of workpeople over the policies and purposes of industry and to arrange for their participation in management.

'The claim to share in the control of industry rests primarily on the simple democratic right of workpeople to have a voice in the determination of their industrial destinies. It is supported by the knowledge that it is only by recognition of this claim that the potentialities, experience, and good sense of the workers can be drawn upon and the full productive powers of industry be effectively realized.'

The 1944 Report outlined the means by which this share in control was to be achieved. Although the members of the board of a nationalized industry should be appointed 'by a Minister responsible to Parliament, and they should, therefore, be selected on the basis of their competence and ability to administer the industry efficiently in the public interest,' the Report also stated that 'statutory provision should be made for the interests of workpeople to be represented on the Governing Board.' This clause was expanded later in the Report to show that it meant that one or two trade union leaders should be appointed to each board, and on appointment should cease to hold office in their union and become responsible to the Minister in exactly the same way as their new colleagues. More important than this, however, was the recommendation that 'consultative machinery, based upon the collective organizations of the workpeople, will be required at all levels; a structure of works, regional or sectional, and national councils from the basic unit up to the Board itself will be necessary. Responsibility for the conduct of units should, however, be clearly defined; though the management must be under an obligation to consult these councils it does not appear that the latter can have any executive authority other than that agreed with the board.'

This second proposal owed much to the success of 'Joint Production Consultative and Advisory Committees' during the second world war. There was nothing in them which went beyond the suggestions of the 1917 Whitley Committee whose reports were followed by the establishment of 'Whitley Councils' in a number of private industries, municipal employment, and the government departments. In the main, however, these councils confined themselves to the traditional business of collective bargaining, and did not encroach far on to recognized 'managerial functions.' The whole purpose of production committees, by contrast, was to advise on matters within the managerial prerogative and during the war many of them could honestly lay claim to both popularity and success. Between the wars 'Whitleyism' had been used as a term of abuse by many trade unionists. Now 'joint consultation' was to be a vehicle for industrial democracy without subverting either efficient management or ministerial and parliamentary responsibility.

The popularity of joint consultation reflected a changed attitude of management towards manpower problems in conditions of full employment and a renewed interest on the part of workers in the control and arrangement of their work now that their jobs were once more relatively secure. The form of nationalization, however, remained the form designed to meet the problems of the 'thirties, to take the big industry-wide decisions which would provide a planned society. Consultative committees perhaps qualified, but certainly did not radically alter, the chosen form. If the industrial democrats were right in thinking that the conflict between liberty and bureaucracy was the major industrial problem, consultative committees were a poor weapon against the massive powers of the boards and the Ministers. By the same token, those who had reacted to the doctrines of industrial democracy by saying that 'workers' control' would mean the domination and exploitation of the consumer by the producer were likely to find cold comfort in the consumers' advisory councils which had also been added to nationalization proposals.

(*c*) *The Ideology of Bigness*

Although the Labour Party and trade unions have become respectable, there is still perhaps a suspicion of oddity, or 'crankiness,' attached to the doctrine of socialism, certainly to the doctrines of industrial democracy. This was far more true during the years after the first world war, when serious support for nationalization, or something very like it, began to come from a highly respectable source, from experienced administrators and from big business itself.

The economic troubles of the period gave strength to a new current of opinion amongst business men on business organization. They began to share American admiration for the giant Corporation, and indeed to go further than the Americans (whose federal laws were still 'anti-trust' in response to a belief in free enterprise and to the voting strength of the small men) in demanding that the government should aid in the process of 'rationalization.' The word 'rationalization' itself became a euphemism for large-scale organization or even straightforward monopoly. Competition, the leading principle of the nineteenth century, began to keep company with the adjective 'wasteful.'

Once the plunge had been taken the converted could see that the advantages of scale were, in theory, almost without limit. The widely recognized advantage that monopolists need not worry overmuch about price-cutting, and can within wide limits ensure that they show a profit, could be slurred over in favour of more generally attractive claims. Planning would become possible. Each unit would be made to fit into a scheme designed to attain the good of the whole organization. Research facilities could be pooled and each unit could benefit from the service of the most highly-skilled technicians whose talents would be made generally available. The managers of the smaller units would no longer feel frustrated. They could look forward, if their merit justified it, to promotion right to the top of the organization. In general, schemes of training and promotion could improve the use of talent throughout the whole organization. On the production side better use could be made both of plant and labour. The structure of prices and of wages could be designed instead of left to the accidents of market forces. Central purchasing would reduce the cost of plant and raw materials, and the financial stability of the whole organization would reduce the cost of raising new funds.

All this, it may be admitted, was not new. The praise bestowed on the socialist methods (though not on the use of the surplus) of the Post Office by Hyndman or Bernard Shaw in the eighteen-eighties found similar virtues in monopoly, and half the socialist case was that competition was 'wasteful.' What was new was the source from which the argument came.

The adherents of bigness were not by any means nationalizers. The greatest of all measures of rationalization, the formation of I.C.I. through the merger of Brunner Mond and Nobel Chemicals, was an achievement of private industry. Even when the state had to be called in, as in the amalgamation of the railway companies under the 1921 Act (which was conceived as an alternative to nationalization), ownership was left to private shareholders and management to their directors. The new railway companies could, of course, be subjected to the rulings of a Railway Rates Tribunal, and the Electricity Commissioners, appointed under an Act of 1919, could be given certain powers (though not enough to accomplish all that was expected of them), because these were services which were used by the general run of owners of productive industry, who wanted to be protected against overcharging, and who stood to gain from the enforcement of standards in electricity supply and distribution. When a new service, the electricity grid system, was to be set up it was perhaps best, especially after the disappointing results of the Commissioners' work (due to their lack of authority to enforce their excellent proposals), to go the whole way to public ownership and entrust the scheme to a board appointed by a Minister. And a similar solution might be accepted for broadcasting, which had proved an awkward business for private concerns from the start, so long as the interests of the radio manufacturers could be adequately protected. It could be argued that broadcasting and the electricity grid were very exceptional cases indeed.

Even if it is admitted, however, that the adherents of bigness were not nationalizers, they certainly made the task of the nationalizer more easy. Lord Ashfield's transport combine had gained control of the majority of London's passenger transport services, but he yearned to lay his hands on the independent bus operators, who, he claimed, were 'creaming off' the traffic and diverting the energies and resources of the combine from developing the kind of transport services which London needed, and could have. He found the restrictions placed upon them by an Act of 1924 insufficient, and sought a further Act which would grant the combine a monopoly. When Herbert Morrison, first as leader of the London Labour Party and then as Minister of Transport in the second Labour Government, demanded that this should only be done under public control, through public ownership and management by a board of the type of the Central Electricity Board, private enterprise could hardly fight this extension of socialism with a clear conscience. The Bill which Morrison drew up and steered through a Joint Committee of Lords and Commons was finally passed, with alterations, by the Conservative-dominated National Government in 1933. A great deal of the credit rightly went to Morrison, but would it have been totally unfair to claim that Lord Ashfield, now become Chairman of the new London Passenger Transport Board, was a *de facto* socialist?

London transport was not the only industry which suffered from wasteful competition during those years. If the colliery companies presented a solid front against nationalization, they welcomed a statutory selling scheme under the 1930 Act. The iron and steel industry claimed that it could set its own house in order with the protection of a tariff, which it got. But in the already much-regulated transport, electricity, and gas industries there were perhaps railway managers or gas and electricity holding company directors faced by obstinate independent companies or untouchable local authority undertakings, who were prepared to do the cause of socialism a service similar to that performed by Lord Ashfield.

Marx taught that 'the historical tendency of capitalist accumulation' was 'the centralization of capital' through the 'progressive diminution of capitalist magnates.' A process near enough to this description went on in America through the trusts and in Germany through cartels, but in Britain nationalization appeared to be a means of fulfilling the historic duty in which the capitalists themselves had failed.

A further argument which told in these industries was the enormous weight of the restrictions of more than half a century of regulative Acts. The future held no prospect of a return to *laissez-faire*. Was not public ownership, which would surely render such detailed control unnecessary, the only method of gaining freedom to get on with the things they wanted to do as they wished to do them?

These considerations turned the thoughts of some business men towards public ownership. But the only form of public ownership which interested them was national ownership. Local authority ownership involved small-scale units which it was their intention to amalgamate, and they wanted management to be by an independent board of experts—perhaps themselves—and not in the hands of a committee of 'butchers and bakers.'

2. The Pragmatic Approach

If private mergers were not forthcoming, only Parliament had authority to enforce action. Parliament was only likely to take an interest when pressed by interested parties, and Parliament's first step was likely to be the setting up of a Royal Commission or Departmental Committee to inquire what action, if any, should be taken (or perhaps to postpone the need for action). The interests of the parties demanding action were likely to be in a particular industry, and so the years between the wars (and the last years of the second world war, when post-war plans were being laid) provide a series of reports on coal, transport, gas, electricity, and civil aviation. Few of the reports favoured nationalization, but most of them recommended further government intervention, and therefore, willy-nilly, tended to provide material for nationalizers. Amongst them the most important for our purposes are, perhaps, the final report of the Royal Commission on Transport (Cmd. 3751 of 1930), the report of the Committee on Electricity Distribution (May, 1936), the report of the Technical Advisory Committee on Coal Mining (Cmd. 6610 of 1945), and the report of the Committee of Inquiry into the Gas Industry (Cmd. 6699 of 1945). (The last three reports are respectively known as the McGowan, Reid, and Heyworth reports, after the names of their chairmen.[1]) These four reports set out to analyse the difficulties and

[1] Lord McGowan was for many years Chairman of I.C.I. Sir Geoffrey Heyworth is Chairman of Unilever. In 1945 Sir Charles Reid was General Manager of the Fyfe Colliery Company. It is interesting to note that the first two chairmen came from the two largest private concerns in the country.

shortcomings of the various industries, and to suggest what might be done about them. They have tended to become the 'compulsory texts' for the boards set up under the post-war nationalization Acts because in them, if anywhere, the boards could find what they were expected to accomplish set out for them in a manner far more helpful than the necessarily general phrases and widely-drawn clauses of the nationalization Acts.

We must deal with each report in turn.

(*a*) *Coal*

By 1945 very few of those with any interest in public affairs doubted that something must be done about the coal industry. The misery of its industrial relations had been by far the most awkward labour problem of the inter-war years, and the direct cause of the General Strike. Declining markets and sagging exports had gone together with a failure to keep up with the increases in output per manshift of our continental rivals. The only reorganization following the 1930 Act had been the district selling schemes, and these, together with the nationalization of royalties under the Coal Act of 1938, had served at the most only to slow the pace of decline. The industry's problems were underlined by the coal shortage, which became as serious as any of the difficulties on the home front during the war. That disaster was avoided was due, in the main, not to the many measures taken by the government to increase production, but to the virtual cessation of exports and to unexpectedly large economies in both the domestic and industrial consumption of coal. That something must be done was generally accepted. The Reid Committee, composed entirely of mining engineers, was set up in September, 1944, to advise the Minister of Fuel and Power on what was needed, and reported the following March.

Their report compared British mining conditions, methods, and production figures with those of some of the most important foreign producers in order to bring out what they felt were the main weaknesses in this country. The second half of the report reviewed almost every aspect of coal-mining in turn and made many detailed recommendations. A considerable number of these concerned systems of mining coal, types of machinery for cutting, loading, and transporting coal underground and to the surface, which might seem to have no necessary connection with ownership or scale of operations. The report found, however, that 'one of the greatest single technical causes of lower O.M.S. in British mines compared with that of the Ruhr or Holland' was their 'use of locomotive haulage on straight level roads . . . instead of the traditional haulage systems used in Britain.' New mines must be sunk and must be designed, where possible, to use continental methods. Many existing mines could with advantage be reconstructed. One of the obstacles was that 'in Britain, the fact that ownership of the mineral has been in private hands has often resulted in unduly small or awkwardly shaped leaseholds; in the development of an excessive number of mines of insufficient capacity for the requirements of the best mining practice; and in inadequate attention to the conservation of national resources.' The transfer of the mineral to the Coal Commission had, because of the conditions attached to it, 'left most of these difficulties still unsolved.' The obstacles to development and reconstruction had been, in part, financial embarrassment and 'uncertainty surrounding the future ownership of the Industry.' Even if these were overcome, however, there remained 'a serious dearth of mining engineers who possess the knowledge and experience necessary to undertake the far-reaching schemes of reorganization which are essential.' Some means of making generally available the abilities of such competent planning engineers as there were would have to be worked out. In order that the 'vast programme of reconstruction of existing mines and the sinking of a number of new ones' could be properly planned, the problem must first be examined by coalfield areas rather than mine by mine; 'the conflicting interests of the individual colliery companies working the area' would have to be 'merged into one compact and unified command of manageable size, with full responsibility, financially and otherwise, for the development of the area'; besides this, 'an Authority must be established which would have the duty of ensuring that the Industry is merged into units of such sizes as would provide the maximum advantages of planned production, of stimulating the preparation and execution of broad plans of reorganization made by these units, and of conserving the coal resources of the country. The existence of such an Authority, endowed by Parliament with really effective powers for these purposes, is, we are satisfied, a cardinal necessity.'

These were not the only recommendations in the report to contain implications for the ownership and organization of the industry. The financing of the huge reconstruction programme was not directly discussed, but there was no likelihood that the necessary funds could be found by the industry itself. The Committee were deeply concerned with the training and education of everyone from the new entrant to the specialist mining engineer, and with systems of promotion, and found that 'an ideal arrangement would be a national scheme.' It might make for economy and efficiency if some surface plants, for example, workshops or coal treatment plants, served 'a number of mines, which may be under different ownership.'

The Committee also turned their attention to the problem of labour relations. They found that 'the problem of securing full co-operation between the employers and the workmen is the most difficult and urgent task the industry has to face,' but it is noteworthy that in this section of their report there is no confident list of recommendations. In their place the Committee put only a moralizing phrase 'that certain rights to which we have suggested the mineworker is entitled must be balanced by a recognition by him of certain duties.'

Although the report did not recommend nationalization, a nationalizer could hardly have hoped for more serviceable ammunition from a committee of experts. He could argue that nationalization would make possible all that the Committee wanted, and that, since nationalization had been demanded by the miners for more than thirty years, it was the only solution to the problem of industrial relations, which the Committee had ranked 'the most difficult and urgent the Industry has to face' and on which they themselves had little to offer.

(*b*) *Electricity*

We have already noted that, as a result of the reports of several committees, the Electricity Commissioners were established in 1919 to co-ordinate the generation and transmission of electricity, an object which, as a result of the excision of compulsory powers from the Bill which constituted them, they had to try to achieve by persuasion. After the report of the Weir Committee in 1925 stronger action was taken through the Electricity (Supply) Act, 1926, which set up the Central Electricity Board to establish the grid, to standardize frequencies as the inter-connection of systems demanded, and to concentrate generation in the most efficient stations. The Electricity Commissioners remained, with the added function of supervising the work of the Board.

These Acts left distribution from the transmission system to the consumer almost untouched. The McGowan Committee was set up in 1935 to inquire into this field, 'to bring under review the organization of the distribution of electricity in Great Britain,' and to make recommendations. In its report of May, 1936, this Committee found two great obstacles to efficiency—the diversity and, in fact, incoherence of the provisions of the various statutory rights and obligations imposed on the industry, and the smallness of the majority of the undertakings. They stated that 'an improvement can and should be effected in the present organization with its numerous undertakings, the widespread duplication of powers, the liability to further disintegration by the exercise of individual local authority purchasing rights and the many and varied systems and voltages of supply and tariffs in operation.'

Some of these shortcomings might be remedied by specific legal changes—for instance, a suspension of local authority rights of purchase, or empowering the Minister of Transport (there was then no Ministry of Fuel and Power) 'to require all undertakers to offer an approved statutory two-part tariff as an optional alternative to a flat rate charge'—but the Committee's main proposal was for area schemes to amalgamate distribution undertakings. This would facilitate the standardization of systems (D.C. or A.C.) and voltages, and of methods of charge; the new organizations would be better able to expand distribution, particularly to rural areas; they would permit a better utilization of capital by spreading loads; that is, by reducing the difference between average load and the peak load which must determine the capacity of the supply and distribution systems. This would be possible because larger areas would be likely to contain a greater diversity of types of demand which would use supplies at different times of day. The Committee considered that the main hope for further reductions in cost lay in better balanced loading. Further advantages of amalgamation would be a reduction in the cost of raising capital, the removal of the reluctance of small undertakings to saddle themselves with the heavy cost of schemes of commercial development, the economies of central purchasing, and the ability of large companies to pay salaries which would attract 'the right type of man with the necessary qualifications' for the chief executive, technical and commercial posts.

The Committee made clear that they did not think that 'adequate grounds' existed 'for an immediate and complete reorganization on a regional basis under public control by the setting up of regional boards.' They proposed instead that the larger and more efficient existing undertakings should be retained, and others absorbed by them. But they stated that 'any attempt to carry through a scheme of reorganization on a voluntary basis is bound to fail and legislation must confer definite and adequate compulsory powers' and that 'schemes of reorganization should make provision for the possibility of ultimate public ownership of all undertakings.'

The Reid Committee had to consider the affairs of an industry already operating, at least for the duration of the war, under a scheme of government direction, and at a time when there was a great 'swing to the left' in the thought of most of the allied countries about the shape of the post-war world. If we remember that the McGowan Committee reported in 1936 we can see that the nationalizer might think its report provided him with plenty of arguments—that the analysis of the industry's problems was sound, but that the remedy suggested fell far short of his own. Moreover, the report dealt only with distribution. The nationalizer argued that generation would never be brought to a high standard of efficiency unless the powers of the Central Electricity Board were completed by bringing the generating stations also under national ownership. He claimed that the statutory regulations under which the Board must buy power from each generating station and sell it back to the distribution undertakings (which might well belong to the company which owned the generating station) fixed tariffs to the advantage of the individual companies and against the interest of the Board and of the nation.

Government proposals following on the McGowan Report caused lively controversy, and were finally shelved when war broke out. By 1945 the industry had added to its difficulties a vast expansion of demand during the war years in which no complementary expansion of generating and distribution facilities was possible—when, in fact, even maintenance and repairs had often to be skimped.

(c) *Gas*

Before nationalization the gas industry was subject to a mass of statutory controls at least as complicated as those which regulated the electricity industry. Moreover, it was the direct competitor of the electricity industry. The latter had all the advantages of coming late into the field, of being able to build in the twentieth century instead of making do with the buildings and equipment of the nineteenth century, together with a rate of technical development far beyond that of the older industry. In these circumstances the gas industry showed its mettle, and fought back remarkably well, especially during the 'thirties, far better than did the railway companies when faced with competition from road transport. The industry had gone after new custom, had developed new appliances for the use of gas, and had screwed up its pitch of efficiency. Its problems, however, were still considered serious enough to warrant the appointment of the Heyworth Committee in 1944 to review them, and to make recommendations.

The Committee concluded that although 'within the limits of its existing structure, the Industry to-day is reasonably efficient . . . the existing structure is restrictive of further progress.' They found that technical efficiency, 'as measured by the proportion of the total available heat energy of the coal appearing as potential heat in the resultant gas and by-products,' was closely related to the size of plant. They thought that considerable economies were possible in transmission systems. They did not think that a national gas grid could be justified, but they were impressed by the savings which could be obtained from local grids, particularly as the result of the more balanced load to be obtained from supplying a wider area and, therefore, a greater variety of consumers, from a single system. Even in areas in which transmission systems had been developed there were still 'too many small inefficient works well within the range of high pressure mains.'

Sales and service to consumers would, they thought, benefit 'by concentration of effort . . . into fewer and stronger hands.' To determine the best types of tariff systems there was need for consumer surveys which 'would involve specialist staffs which are beyond the resources of many of the units of the Industry.' Statutory price and dividend control were restrictive, more so in fact than in the electricity industry, since there rapid technical progress had made statutory maximum prices irrelevant. 'A solution must be found which will permit the abolition rather than the perpetuation of these controls.' There was need for standardization of statistics and, at least by regions, of gas qualities.

Reorganization into larger units could improve the conditions of work of those employed in smaller undertakings by making possible the introduction of labour-saving machinery beyond the means of these undertakings (so long as they remained independent). Performance could be improved by training, but adequate training schemes again were beyond the means of small undertakings. Limited by its existing structure, the industry offered 'too little scope for first-class men to attain to positions commensurate with their abilities,' and the salaries of executive and administrative staff, particularly in municipal undertakings, compared unfavourably with 'those paid in other industries for work of equal responsibility.'

Large units were required. No satisfactory scheme of amalgamation was likely to be achieved by voluntary action because of the basic structural difference between the companies and the municipal undertakings. Further company fusions and more municipal joint boards were not in themselves very hopeful lines of advance, and could not 'produce a pattern of grouping even approximating to the ideal.' The existing undertakings must, therefore, be bought out by Parliament. Since no important problems of the industry were nation-wide, the management of the industry should be entrusted to Regional Boards set up by Act of Parliament.

The Committee described in some detail the organization which they hoped would be adopted for the Boards. Their main aim was to place responsibility 'squarely on the shoulders of the Boards' and they, therefore, did not propose 'advisory panels of experts or of consumers or a standing co-ordinating Committee of Regional Board Chairmen.' The members of the Boards were to be appointed by the Minister of Fuel and Power who would be responsible 'for decision as to the success or failure of the Boards' and in a position 'analogous to that of the shareholding body in a limited company.'

Regional organization would have the advantage (and this argument also applied to electricity) of placing a clear responsibility on one Board or another for 'initiating any new development which is found to be commercially desirable' in any part of the country. Previously a given locality might have been without a service because no undertaking would admit responsibility for it.

The proposals of the Heyworth Committee were more radical than those of the McGowan Report. The differences between the problems of the two industries do not seem to provide any good reason for this.

If an explanation is wanted, it might be found partly in the composition of the two Committees, but mainly, perhaps, in the change in social and political environment between 1936 and 1945.

(*d*) *Transport*

Railway legislation bulked large amongst the activities of Parliament in the nineteenth century. The Act of 1921 under which the companies were amalgamated was only one chapter in a long story of public regulation. Like another much-regulated industry, the gas industry, railways had to face a youthful competitor, road transport; but unlike the gas industry's competitor —electricity—which Parliament regulated from the start, road transport was for many years allowed to develop much as it wished, or as market forces directed. The railways suffered severely and were only too willing to make their sufferings known to the public and to Parliament. Accordingly one of the main tasks of the Royal Commission on Transport, which was set up by the Conservative Government of 1928 and continued to sit under the second Labour Government, was to consider what measures, if any, should be taken to co-ordinate the various means of transport. Their final report, published in December, 1930, entitled, 'The Co-ordination and Development of Transport,' was mainly concerned with this question. The Commissioners thus had to consider two different problems, first the internal efficiency of the various sections of transport, and secondly their relationship to each other. It was as if they had to perform the tasks of the Reid, Heyworth, and McGowan Committees, and, on top of that, make recommendations for the co-ordination of fuel and power.

The Commission felt that the railway companies had not done all they could to meet road competition. They remarked that there had been almost 'no improvement in locomotive speed in this country during the last eighty years' and felt something could be done about it. A general revision and lowering of fares would attract custom. In many ways poor service was offered both to passengers and to traders. All suburban services should be electrified. An earlier report (Cmd. 3416 of 1929) had made recommendations on the regulation of road passenger transport vehicles. The Commission now turned their attention to road haulage, and recommended that vehicles should be licensed by the Area Traffic Commissioners. These Commissioners should have regard only to the fitness of vehicles and the wages and conditions of employees, but registration would put the industry 'on an organized basis' and be an essential preliminary to any general co-ordination. The Commission thought that trams were now obsolete and should ultimately be abolished. They did not despair of a useful future for some canals and inland waterways, but felt that only by amalgamation could a development programme be made possible. Failing the submission of voluntary schemes 'within a short period' they were prepared to recommend that the Minister of Transport should set up Public Trusts to acquire 'such canals as he considers it would be in the national interest to preserve and improve.'

These, together with some observations on docks and harbours, and a long section on highways, constitute the main recommendations of the Commission relating to separate sections of the transport industry. On co-ordinating the sections they could not agree. The only recommendation which they could put forward as a body was that a small permanent Advisory Council should be set up to study transport problems, and to make recommendations to the Minister of Transport.

The Commissioners were agreed that 'without unification . . . no attempt to bring about complete co-ordination would be successful.' They thought unification might be achieved by 'nationalization' (by which they meant ownership and operation by a government department), 'rationalization' (by which they meant a merger into one vast private combine), Parliamentary acquisition of property to be leased to private operators, or the formation of a Public Transport Trust (which meant, as reference to the B.B.C. and the Central Electricity Board showed, a public corporation). The final paragraphs of their report related that some of them held strongly that conscious co-ordination, either by 'nationalization' or by a Public Trust, was desirable; whereas others were opposed to government action, believing that no further steps should be taken beyond those already recommended in the report, and 'that such further co-ordination of the various forms of transport as may be advantageous will come about naturally through the play of economic forces.' They claimed that they would watch 'with very great interest' the operation of London Transport if the plans announced by the government for its unification were carried out.

Although all the members of the Commission signed the report, there were two reservations, an additional memorandum, and a document containing additional recommendations from three of the Commissioners. This last definitely recommended 'a real policy of rationalization through the purchase of the properties of the railway companies, of the motor transport services, and of such canals as may be deemed to be essential parts of a national scheme, and the creation of a National Transport Trust to which should be delegated by the State the duty of managing on commercial lines the unified undertakings.' If this were not done, there would be 'an over supply of facilities, but through the cost of rivalries and the absence of complete co-ordination, rates, freight charges and fares will not be cheap.' They thought that 'if the present transport rivalries were left to work themselves out it is highly probable that some of the railway undertakings, without State protection, will be unable to pay their way. This is a contingency which ought to be avoided.'

If the success of co-ordination was to be judged by an easing of the financial difficulties of the railways, the years following the Commission's report did not show any signs of natural co-ordination through 'the play of economic forces.' Further regulation of road transport, through the Commission's licensing scheme, through heavier taxation, through the Road Haulage Wages Act, 1938, and through the provision for the railways of special facilities for raising cheap capital for development, did not answer the railways' problem. As the British economy climbed out of depression their finances improved slowly only to slip back disastrously in the two years immediately before the war, so that the companies undertook to acquaint the public with their plight and the need for remedy by widespread advertisement of their demand for 'a square deal.' Accordingly nationalizers concluded that 'economic forces' had failed and argued that the only other means thought possible by the Commission—'co-ordination through unification'—ought to be adopted forthwith.

One point on transport nationalization is worthy of note. The argument for co-ordination may be a pragmatic argument, but it is by no means as easy to handle as, say, the argument that the lay-out of mines ought not to be determined by the accident of leaseholds, or the argument that the service of wider areas would improve the load factor in electricity and gas. This is so because it is not easy to ascribe a clear and definite meaning to the word 'co-ordination.' The 'Additional Recommendations' of the three members of the Royal Commission accepted the definition offered by a witness 'a condition in which two or more systems, whether in the same or separate ownership, work together efficiently under an arrangement mutually agreed and conditioned by the public interest.' This only shrouds the question in further mystery. There is little in the whole report to guide the puzzled to a better understanding of the word, or, indeed, to demonstrate that the members of the Commission understood it themselves.

(*e*) *Air Transport*

It is difficult to fit the two other industries which were the subjects of post-war nationalization Acts—air transport and iron and steel—into the pattern which we have been trying to build up.

With the former our defence is not difficult. The British Overseas Airways Act was passed in 1939 and the first Board of the new Corporation took over from Imperial Airways on April 1, 1940. Post-war Acts have reorganized the industry, but it was already nationalized. In many ways it is more analogous to the B.B.C. than to the group of industries which have been nationalized since 1945. Almost from the start it was generally admitted that the industry was peculiarly 'affected with the public interest.' There were two reasons for this. First of all the development of the aircraft industry was for military reasons a matter of national concern. To a considerable extent, however, development was dependent on civilian orders. Air lines must, therefore, pay attention to military as well as to commercial considerations in planning and ordering aircraft. Secondly, the development and maintenance of a widespread network of routes was a matter of imperial politics and national prestige, before which commercial considerations might again have to give way. The advantages of large-scale operation had been appreciated long before nationalization, and

Imperial Airways had been set up as a private monopoly, which would nevertheless have regard for public policy in return for a subsidy to cover losses thereby incurred. The primary reason for nationalization was not, therefore, the desire to remedy internal inefficiency, or to change a structure which hampered further progress, but a widespread feeling that the arrangement with Imperial Airways did not permit sufficient attention to be paid to national needs. These would only be granted the hearing they deserved if the industry was transferred to public ownership, and operated by a Board appointed by the Minister and subject to his directions. The industry was, like broadcasting, one which a party committed to the doctrine of private enterprise was prepared to admit to be an exception to its own generalizations.

(*f*) *Steel*

Steel is most certainly not in the same category as air transport. It found its way into the Labour Party's immediate nationalization programme during the depression of 1929–33, when the Labour movement, looking at Jarrow and the shipyard breaking activities of Shipbuilding Securities Limited, and at South Wales and the other depressed areas, yearned for the power to make a radical change, the power with which it thought unemployment could be planned away. Control of the banks and investment was perhaps the first step, but control of steel was at least as important for national planning as control of fuel and power or transport.

It is true that at that time the internal state of the

industry was by no means happy. Technically backward compared with the steel industries of the United States, Germany, Belgium, or even France, it was showing itself less and less able to defend even the domestic market from foreign competition. Financially embarrassed, with a very heavy rate of unemployment amongst its workers, it made loud demands for a tariff as the necessary prerequisite of any attempt to put its own house in order. At that time there seemed to be every reason for nationalizers to classify it with the mines or the railways.

From 1932, however, the industry had the protection of a tariff in return for a promise of reorganization. The industry set up the Iron and Steel Federation as a cartel, and the arrangements made by the Federation, together with returning prosperity and the beginnings of rearmament, allayed its financial worries. The Labour Party has argued that reorganization ought to have meant development rather than monopolistic restrictions, and took the view that new plants at Ebbw Vale and Corby represented an effort which fell far short of the nation's need. During the war steel was in short supply, but this was not regarded as an urgent public problem, threatening disaster, like the coal shortage. After the war the industry readily admitted the need for development, and produced a Federation plan which was dependent on government financial assistance. The plan and the obligation to provide assistance was accepted by the government, which set up a public board to supervise the carrying out of the suggested projects.

A strong case for nationalization could still be made

out. It was argued that in the depression the 'steel barons had held the country to ransom.' They had got their tariff and had then reorganized their selling methods in their own interests. It was argued that public financing of the post-war plan should be accompanied by public control, which could only be fully effective under public ownership. Some socialist writers condemned the plan as altogether inadequate to provide the quantity of steel which the rebuilding of Britain and the re-equipping of British industry would require. Steel was a basic industry and its nationalization was essential if the government was to plan the British economy. Finally, nationalization of steel was part of the Labour Government's programme.

Steel, then, is an exception because there was no general agreement, fostered by public inquiries and reports, that essential development could not be carried out without compulsory reorganization of the industry. The technical needs of the industry and the means of meeting them were not laid down in the report of a Royal Commission or a Departmental Committee, but in a report prepared by the Iron and Steel Federation itself, and accepted by the government. It was exceptional in that, by commercial standards, it was doing very well indeed. It was not hampered by the volume of regulations which in gas and electricity made nationalization seem a means of gaining liberty of action. It was not, like the coal industry, patently failing to supply the nation's needs. It most certainly refrained from washing its dirty linen in public as the transport industry was prone to do. Large sections of the gas and electricity industry and of road passenger transport were already publicly

D

owned by local authorities. The railways and the mines had been operated by the government during the two wars. The steel industry was unquestionably private industry, and steel employers and managers showed quite clearly that they wished it to remain private. There was less of the pragmatic approach to steel than in any other instance of nationalization, but steel nationalization was a conflict between socialism and capitalism far more than were they.

3. The Public Corporation

If we write of departmental operation, operation by a public corporation, and 'workers' control' as three different methods of nationalization, we should not give the impression that they are entirely distinct. The National Guild of the industrial democrats, for instance, might have been a public corporation, although a public corporation with a membership vastly greater than that of the B.B.C. or the Central Electricity Board. Workers' control and departmental operation were confused in proposals for 'joint control,' such as that contained in the Bill drafted for the Miners' Federation in 1919; and it was easy for critics to suggest that conflicts and dual loyalties were likely to arise in a board consisting partly of trade union representatives responsible to their unions and partly of government nominees under the chairmanship of a departmental minister.

Hybrids are possible; but there is no doubt that the public corporation, which had outdistanced its competitors by 1930, was popularly understood to be quite distinct from them. Its success was partly due to its supposed freedom from the shortcomings attributed to them, for this recommended it to those businessmen and administrators who were convinced of the need for rationalization, and who had come to think that the obstacles to voluntary action were so great that public ownership was the only way forward. They thought of workers' control as a dangerous, or more likely a silly and irresponsible, slogan of the lunatic fringe. Many businessmen had experienced departmental control during the first world war, and had disliked what they described as its bureaucracy, delay, and red tape. What they wanted was more power for themselves to do what they thought was required. If Parliament would acquire all the assets of their own industry and appoint them to be members of a board to manage those assets, they would have power. If there had to be nationalization, then, for them, the public corporation was unquestionably the best method.

They could receive some support even from the advocates of workers' control. Before the Sankey Commission, and elsewhere, industrial democrats had made use of all the anti-bureaucratic objections that businessmen had found against departmental operation. The doctrine of industrial democracy had arisen, in part, out of a revolt against bureaucratic socialism. And at least the public corporation would avoid detailed parliamentary and ministerial control.

Support from this quarter was perhaps unimportant, for after 1920 syndicalist tendencies were losing their hold on the Labour movement. Parliamentary socialists might be expected to see freedom from parliamentary control as a weakness of the public corporation, for it would reduce their control over industry, their power to plan. Conservative spokesmen for the Electricity Supply Bill (under which, when passed, the Central Electricity Board was set up) claimed that a public corporation was not nationalization at all. The industry would be run by its own experts, they said, and not by Civil Servants; its operations would be free from parliamentary inquiry and from the 'dead hand' of Treasury control. Small wonder that Labour's then expert on the organization of the electricity industry, Major Attlee, replied that his party thought that popular control through Parliament was a virtue.

Much of the credit for changing the mind of the Labour Party must go to Herbert Morrison's defence of the independent board of experts during the controversy over the London Passenger Transport Bill. And the logic of his case could be supported by the sensible political calculation that, since the public corporation had already become acceptable to a large number of people who were by no means socialists, the best thing for socialists who thought of nationalization as the primary aim, and the form as secondary, was to advocate nationalization by means of the public corporation. The failures of the first two Labour Governments had convinced the Labour movement that its next government must act, and made it more interested in what was practical than in preserving sterile doctrinal purity.

What was the public corporation? Before 1945 the most important examples were the B.B.C., the Central Electricity Board, and the London Passenger Transport Board. Although the Port of London Authority (established under an Act of 1908) was often coupled with them, it was a very different institution and had more in common with harbour authorities in other parts of the country than with the inter-war corporations, even though it was cited by Conservative ministers as a precedent for the B.B.C. and the Central Electricity Board. British Overseas Airways, established in 1940, had not had time to make its mark.

The public corporation was, then, a board usually of less than ten members, endowed with legal personality, and charged with running a business enterprise. It was not expected to make a profit, but it was expected to cover all its costs. At first glance it might seem that the company director would find himself in a familiar situation if translated to the board, but there were some important differences between the public corporation and the public company.

It would be admitted by all that the B.B.C. was a special case. Its income came from licence fees regarded by the Treasury as part of the revenue, and it took its duties as an educational service seriously. So that the motives for its actions were not the same as those of the ordinary business enterprise. Apart from this, however, there were other differences. The public corporations were statutory monopolies and could not appear to the consumer as competitive concerns. Although the device of appointing trustees was adopted by the Conservatives in their final draft of Morrison's London Passenger Transport Bill to emphasize freedom from political control, Parliament could not pretend it had no responsibility for a monopoly which it had established, and an appointing minister, do as he would, could not look like a body of shareholders. Moreover, an Act of Parliament was not the same as articles of association.[1]

The willingness of Parliament and ministers to leave the corporations alone during the inter-war years minimized these differences at the time, but the attitude of Parliament might change, and it did. Conservative opinion had altered enough by 1939 to subject British Overseas Airways to direct ministerial control in a number of matters, for one of the main reasons for taking over Imperial Airways was the lack of co-operation between that company and government departments—the exercise of the 'independence' which had been valued so highly in 1926 and 1933. To many members of the Labour Party ministerial control was a matter of principle. During the depression they had discovered that the government had no powers to force the public corporations to expand in order to relieve unemployment. They had accepted the public corporation but they could not accept so great a degree of independence; on such terms what value had nationalization to them?

In their Interim Report on Post-War Reconstruction, the General Council of the T.U.C. held that:

'It will be necessary also to provide for the ultimate responsibility of the managements of socialized industries to a Minister in order to ensure the proper co-ordination of their policies and that the industries are conducted in full accordance with the Govern-

[1] For a further discussion of these points see *Management and Accountability in the Nationalized Industries* by D. N. Chester, a paper read to the Manchester Statistical Society, 9th January, 1952.

ment's general plans for the maintenance of employment, the control and location of industry, and the furtherance of socially desirable expansion of production.'

Consequently, the post-war public corporations differed from their predecessors not only in the wider scope of their monopolies and in the vastly greater numbers of their employees, but also in their relationship with Parliament. The Acts gave the appropriate Minister specific authority over certain aspects of their work and over-all power to give directions 'of a general character.' The Central Electricity Board and the London Passenger Transport Board lost their former status by incorporation in the British Electricity Authority and the Transport Commission.

The public corporation, as we know it to-day, is a legacy of the inter-war years. It is a development of the corporations established in those years to overcome the faults which the Labour movement thought their experience revealed.

. . . . .

If we may pretend that history can be divided up into neat periods with separate labels, we can divide the development of the thought of the Labour movement on nationalization into four sections.

Up to the first years of the present century socialists were mainly concerned with the problem of poverty. They wanted nationalization in order to reduce inequality in incomes and to permit the planning which would give work to all and increase the national dividend. They were so convinced of the importance of their general principles, and so occupied with the business of propagating them, that they gave little thought to the mechanisms through which nationalization would be applied to industry.

The industrial democrats gave their attention less to benefits to the consumer than to the freedom and happiness of the producer. During the first world war, workers, relatively secure in their jobs, showed interest in improving their status at work, and in using their power as producers to do so. They listened readily to the teachings of the industrial democrats, but, despite attempts to elaborate the guild system, few gave much thought to the institutions through which 'workers' control' could be made effective.

With returning unemployment poverty once more became the central problem and men looked to Parliament once more for its relief. In this period, however, detailed plans were laid for action, including nationalization of the basic industries. The public corporation, which was already being used to achieve desirable development in certain cases in which voluntary action was ineffective, was taken over by the planners to serve the same purpose on a larger scale—in major industries—and was adapted to work also as a mechanism for national planning.

By the time that this new model could be put into production, conditions akin to those of the second period had returned. There had already been several years of full employment, and poverty had been relieved, if not overcome, by considerable changes in the distribution of the national income. Labour shortage had made effective labour utilization one of the first concerns of the employer, and had turned the attention of the worker away from finding a job in order to eat towards the task of making his working life more satisfactory to him. It was in these conditions that large-scale use was made for the first time of the instrument developed in the inter-war period.

Chapter II

THE ORGANIZATION OF NATIONALIZED INDUSTRY

THE original British Overseas Airways Corporation took over on 1st April, 1940, under an Act of 1939. This Act has since been modified by the Civil Aviation Act, 1946 (under which the British European Airways Corporation and the British South American Airways Corporation were also established), and the Air Corporations Act, 1949 (under which B.S.A.A.C. was merged with B.O.A.C.). The dates of royal assent to the post-war Acts with which we are concerned, and of the respective vesting days, are as follows:

	Royal Assent	*Vesting Date*
Coal – –	12th July, 1946	1st Jan., 1947
Electricity –	13th Aug., 1947	1st April, 1948
Gas – –	30th July, 1948	1st May, 1949
Transport –	6th Aug., 1947	1st Jan., 1948
Iron and Steel –	24th Nov., 1949	15th Feb., 1951

The Acts had much to say about the process of transfer to public ownership, about the general duties and financial methods of the proposed boards, and about the framework of national organization and in some instances also regional organization. They left over the construction of the lower storeys of the new buildings on which these superstructures would have to rest.

The task of completing the plans and of erecting the building was entrusted to the new board, whose appointment was the Minister's first concern after the passage of the Act, or to an Organizing Committee set up during the passage of the Act, whose members were almost all subsequently appointed to the board. The way they did their work was influenced by the need to build their organization around going concerns (which included employers' organizations, research organizations, and other bodies which served the industry as a whole, as well as productive units and companies) without interrupting their work. They were also, naturally, influenced by the prevalent ideas about the organization of the industries concerned which have been outlined in the last chapter. Most of the members of the boards (and of the Committees which preceded them) were either company directors or senior executives from the industries which were being nationalized. Ex-trade union officials made the second largest group. Next came a few senior Civil Servants who were expected to provide expert knowledge on methods of organization. Given this composition, the task to be performed, and the brief time allowed, it is neither surprising nor culpable that the first concern of the boards and committees was to devise an organization which could get to work quickly, rather than to think far ahead.

Since each group was trying to construct an organization to suit its own industry, we must first describe the outcome of the work of each in turn, and leave until later the examination of the common problems which have been thrown up.

1. Coal

(a) *The Growth of Organization*

Unlike the later Transport, Electricity, and Gas Acts, the Coal Nationalization Act made no provision for subordinate bodies through which the National Coal Board was to operate the undertakings which passed into its ownership. The Act thus left the Organizing Committee and later the Board free to devise whatever organization should seem to them to fit the needs of the industry and to enable them to carry out their general duties as laid down by the Act. Several considerations were, however, bound to affect their planning.

About 1,500 collieries were transferred to the Board. They had previously been owned by 746 colliery undertakings. Some of these undertakings were in the hands of individuals and partnerships, but the great majority, about 640, were limited companies. Four hundred and ninety small undertakings produced less than 100,000 tons a year. Although the remaining 250-odd undertakings produced the bulk of the country's output, few of them could be called large concerns. Only fifty-one of them produced more than 1,000,000 tons a year each, and of these only seven more than 3,000,000 tons each. Perhaps a dozen companies employed specialist officers, such as electrical and mechanical engineers, and only a few of these, for instance, Powell Duffryn and the Fife Coal Company, had a formal organization for the control of its constituent collieries which would bear comparison with those normally used in large modern industrial undertakings.

The Coal Board did not take over the colliery undertakings, many of which ramified into all manner of other activities besides producing coal. It took over only certain assets. Those assets of the undertaking which were concerned with coal production were already listed and valued under the 'profit-sharing' wage agreement of 1921 which prescribed that the proceeds of the industry, after minimum wages and all other costs had been paid, should be divided, district by district, between profits and wages in a fixed ratio. These assets were compulsorily transferred. Of the other assets of the colliery undertakings, some could be transferred at the option of the undertakings, some at the option of the Board, and some by agreement.

Four hundred of the 1,500 collieries acquired by the Board were classified as 'small mines' and operated privately under licence from the Board. Even so, to make any kind of control effective the Board had to find some means of grouping together the remaining collieries. The company structure could not be used for this purpose for two reasons. The Board took over assets, not companies; and the company structure provided adequate grouping in only one or two areas.

It had often been assumed—for instance, in the schemes for nationalization prepared by the Miners' Federation, or those presented in the various reports of the Sankey Commission (1919)—that the district would be used for this purpose. The boundaries of the districts, twenty-five in number, had originally been defined by the organization of the miners and of the colliery owners, and by the wage agreements which they made. With some rearrangement, they were used for the selling schemes established under the Coal Mines Act of 1930.

There was, however, a great variation in size between the districts. Their range of production was from a few hundred thousand tons a year to twenty-five million. Few of them were well suited to serve as the 'compact and unified command of manageable size' asked for by the Reid Report.

Under the wartime Coal Control, which continued until vesting day, the headquarters organization in the Ministry of Fuel and Power worked through regions. For distributing and 'programming' coal the whole country was divided into twelve regions; eight of these were 'producing' regions with responsibilities for the production of coal, and coincided with boundaries originally established for the mines inspectorate.

The Coal Board have made it quite clear that their choice of unit for grouping was based on the same technical considerations as those that swayed the Reid Committee. In their Annual Report of 1948 they say:

'The National Coal Board had decided in 1946, before the industry passed into national ownership, that the headquarters of colliery companies were to be merged into compact areas under General Managers and that under nationalization the Areas were to be the main units of business management. The number and size of the Areas were not matters of speculation or rule of thumb. The facts of geography and geology spoke for themselves as did the experiences of the larger companies in the industry which had secured increased efficiency by concentrating management in large units.'

They went on to say that 'Areas were not made so

large that they could not conveniently be supervised by the Area General Manager,' quoting the recommendations of the Reid Report in support.

One of the reasons for rejecting organization by districts had apparently been the view of the Board that twenty-five units were beyond the reasonable span of control of one national body. If this was so, organization into areas, which would of necessity break up the larger districts into several units, would render the Board's task even more difficult. Accordingly, it was decided to insert an additional storey into the building. The eight producing regions of the wartime Control were adapted for this purpose into eight divisions, each of which was to have a Divisional Board, appointed by the National Board.

The boundaries of these divisions corresponded fairly well with the coalfields and with the traditional groupings of the industry. There was one Scottish Division. The Northern Division grouped together Durham, Northumberland, and Cumberland. The North-Western Division included Lancashire and North Wales. Yorkshire had a division to itself—the North-Eastern. Derby, Nottingham, and Leicester came into the East Midlands; Stafford, Shropshire, and Warwickshire into the West Midlands. Somerset was grouped with South Wales in the South-Western Division, and the small Kent coalfield had a South-Eastern Division of its own. Apart from this last division, which was a pygmy compared to the others, the size of the divisions in 1947 ranged, in numbers of wage-earners on colliery books, from the Northern, with an average over the year of 156,000, to the West Midlands, with 59,000; and in output, from the

North-Eastern, with 37·4 million tons over the year, to the North-Western, with 12·6 million.

As soon as the Divisional Boards were appointed, they and the National Board set about mapping out the areas. The South-Eastern Division was not subdivided. The other divisions were split up into forty-eight areas. Some of these areas corresponded to the old districts. The two smallest districts (Somerset and Bristol) were amalgamated into one area, many of the larger districts were split up into two or more areas, and sometimes it was thought best to cross district boundaries in order to mark out an administratively viable unit.

The 1948 Annual Report of the Coal Board says of the areas:

'In fact, the sizes of the Areas vary and the coal each produces may be anything from ½ million tons to 7 million tons. There had to be small Areas to look after groups of collieries which were separated by long distances from other collieries, and there are many Areas extending over wide territory having only a small output because the collieries within it are few, small and scattered. The average Area, however, has an output of about 4 million tons and a turnover of about £10 million; the number of men employed is about 16,000.'

The average number of pits in an area is twenty, and the range is from sixty-six in Area No. 1 (anthracite) of the South-Western Division to six pits in Area No. 7 of the same division.

Looking at their span of command, many of the area managers shared the attitude of the National Board when it decided against direct control of twenty-five districts or forty-eight areas. Many areas were, therefore, divided up into sub-areas, with sub-area managers responsible to the area manager; and in some sub-areas agents were appointed (following the practice of the larger colliery companies) to be responsible to the sub-area manager for a group of three or four pits.

Besides this geographical division of the industry a division of functions had to be arranged. The wartime Coal Control, in which some of the members of the Board had served, had four departments—Labour, Finance, Production, and Marketing—and four corresponding directorates in each of its producing regions. The Coal Board adopted the same arrangements, but split the Labour Department into two, entitled Labour Relations and Manpower and Welfare. One reason for this change was that the main responsibility of the first department would be for collective bargaining on wages and conditions with the unions. Manpower was clearly one of the industry's most difficult problems, and it was thought undesirable to run the risk that consideration of it or of welfare matters should be swamped by the business of collective bargaining.

To these 'ready-made' departments the Board added a Scientific Department, a Legal Department, and a Secretary's Department. Scientific research and control were of major importance to a Board with statutory responsibility for 'the efficient development of the coal-mining industry.' The two last-named departments provided services which had been performed for the wartime Control by the Ministry of Fuel and Power; separate arrangements had now to be made. The Secretary's Department was the most important innovation. Working mainly to the deputy chairman,

Sir Arthur Street, it was intended to provide unifying direction to the diverse elements of the industry.

These departments were duplicated at the division and, with the general exception of the Legal Department and with some other local variations,[1] at the area.

Once the geographical and functional divisions had been planned, they had to be fitted together. In their account of their organization given in their Annual Report for 1948 the Coal Board explained that the method it chose 'is the one usually adopted by large organizations. It is based on the principle of "Line and Staff."' The line of command, and of personal (or collective) responsibility, runs from the National Board through the Divisional Boards and area managers to the colliery managers. The departmental chiefs and their assistants constitute the staff, and as such 'carry out specialist duties' for the responsible manager or board, 'perform common services,' and 'act as a clearing house for the collection and dissemination of technical information.' 'All general instructions pass between the authorities in the Line,' who, therefore, 'have responsibility for major decisions' and 'can be judged on their results.' 'Technical advice and guidance' through staff channels avoids 'overburdening the Line authorities with a mass of technical detail, and permits economies to be reaped from organizing consultancy and other services on a common basis.'

As the members of the Coal Board would readily admit, the enunciation of a principle of this kind does not of itself resolve the problem. We must look more

[1] Some areas, for instance, have amalgamated Labour and Welfare.

closely at the detailed arrangements to see how the principle was applied.

The members of the National Board were intended to have dual responsibility. Apart from the chairman, each member had individual responsibility for a headquarters department as well as collective responsibility for the control of the 'Line.' Appointments were made with this intention. The deputy chairman came from the Civil Service. The Labour and Welfare members came from trade unions. A physics professor, an accountant, and a director of coal-distributing companies took responsibility for science, finance, and marketing. Two mining engineers, who had previously been directors of colliery companies, went to the Production Department. The 1948 Report explained:

'At that time there was really no choice; no staff had yet been appointed and the Members of the Board themselves had to get down to the job of organizing the departments because there was no one else to do it for them.'

The report goes on to argue that in a ' "policy" board composed only of non-specialist administrators there is always the feeling the technicians are being overruled by people who do not understand technical matters,' to refer to the governing bodies of the services and of the Post Office as examples of functional boards, and to quote Mr. Winston Churchill's stated preference for dealing with 'chiefs of organizations rather than counsellors.'

The Divisional Boards followed much the same pattern. A Chairman (chosen from outside the industry) and a Deputy Chairman (from within the industry) shared responsibility with Divisional Directors of Production, Finance, Marketing, and Labour. The other departments, however, had no direct representation on the boards.

The area general managers were at first expected to act as their own production managers. In their Annual Report for 1947 the Coal Board explained that they 'had appointed as Area General Managers highly qualified mining engineers . . . because of the importance of increasing coal production at once and of planning the technical reconstruction of the collieries.' This arrangement could not be readily squared with 'Line and Staff' principles. The area general manager 'was Chairman of the Area Management Committee.' For 'production matters he was responsible to the Divisional Production Director, and on other matters to the Chairman of the Divisional Board.' The report emphasized that the arrangement was not ideal, and had been regarded from the outset as an experiment.

Although the colliery manager might have some specialist assistants, these would usually be no more than clerical staff and a few craftsmen. The Reid Report had recognized the lack of specialists and the need for making their services generally available. Accordingly, the colliery manager was to rely on the area for their services. His relation to the 'Staff' was thus very different from that of the superior Line authorities. Their staff services came from their assistants; his from the assistants of his superior.

Between the colliery and the area there might be both agents and a sub-area organization. The position of agents was clear. They were responsible to the area manager for groups of pits in order to enable the latter to exercise his control more easily; but their responsibility was only for the functions exercised by the colliery managers themselves. The authority of the sub-area manager was not so easily defined. He was to be something more than a 'glorified agent' and some specialist services have been attached to the sub-area; but his command was not usually a separate 'unified command' such as the area was intended to be.

In any organization there are odd pieces not easily fitted into a simple pattern, and the Coal Board is no exception. It took over from colliery companies manufactured fuel plants, carbonization and by-product plants, brickworks, farms, and other land, nearly 150,000 houses and many other buildings, and a great variety of miscellaneous assets. Main-line wagons were transferred to the Transport Commission in 1948, but the other assets and several independent organizations such as the Coal Commission, the Coal Survey, and the staff of the Miners' Welfare Commission (which remained an independent organization, but handed over all its administrative functions) had to be attached, as seemed most convenient, to areas, divisions, or the National Board, thereby increasing their responsibilities and adding to the numbers of their staff.

(*b*) *Changes in Organization*

Before the end of their first year the Coal Board decided that the arrangement whereby area general managers acted as their own production managers should not be continued. New production managers should be appointed to the area general managers' staffs, and 'the new post of Area General Manager was to carry full responsibility for Area management in all its aspects.'

This change could not by itself allay the widespread criticism of the administration of the industry which came to a head in May, 1948, when Sir Charles Reid resigned from the Board almost at the same time as the Board announced that it had appointed a committee 'to look into the organization of the coal industry.' Two of the committee's members came from outside the industry, one of them, Sir Charles Renold, being Chairman of the British Institute of Management; the third, the chairman, was Sir Robert Burrows, who had recently become a part-time member of the Board. The brief 'Main Recommendations' of its report, together with the comments of the Coal Board, were published by the Board, and may be found in an appendix to the Annual Report for 1948. There were no revolutionary proposals, for the report approved the structure of the organization. Several suggestions, such as the inclusion of divisional chairmen in the National Board, were rejected. Some, for instance, the transfer of marketing from areas to divisions, were accepted. The next to last recommendation of the report stated, starkly and without qualification, that: 'The position of Colliery Managers should be strengthened.' No means to this end were suggested.

The Burrows Committee also recommended that the Board 'should be enlarged by the addition of a second Deputy Chairman and up to three part-time members' and that members 'in charge of functional Departments, while retaining responsibility for their Departments, should leave executive action to their chief officials.' This reflected a growing antipathy to the functional board, revealed in criticisms of the Coal Board, in the arrangements made under later nationalization Acts, and in changes in the Coal Board itself, despite the Board's defence of functional responsibility quoted above.[1] The comments of the Board show that the first point had been 'mooted before the Committee was set up' and legislation was pending,[2] and that 'the practice of leaving executive action to senior departmental officials has been steadily developing. . . . Only four of the nine Members of the Board now have responsibility for a department.'

The transfer of marketing from areas to divisions seems to have been a useful change, but even now there is duplication of staff and effort in the non-producing ('white') areas of the country, and it may be that the Coal Board would do well to add to its territorial divisions a separate functional organization for marketing to cover the whole country. The divisional boards would then be responsible only for production.

Resignations, deaths, and retirements in 1951, when the contracts of the original Board fell in, have almost completely altered the personnel of the Board. Two members, including the new chairman, Sir Hubert Houldsworth, have come from the divisions. The only members who retain departmental responsibilities are the members responsible for Labour and Welfare and the Scientific member; and the part-time members include some of the most famous of British businessmen, such as Sir Geoffrey Heyworth of Unilever, who would not have been likely to accept a full-time appointment.

[1] See page 57.

[2] The Coal Industry Act, 1949, allowed the Minister to increase the total number of members of the Board from nine to twelve, of whom not more than eight (apart from the chairman) should render whole-time service.

At the end of 1949 the Coal Board decided to split its Northern Division into two, separating Durham (the largest coalfield) from Northumberland and Cumberland. In its report for that year the Board explained the change by reference to 'big problems, both technical and economic, in the Northern coalfields,' instancing Durham's thin seams, the exhaustion of reserves in part of Northumberland, and Cumberland's isolation and high costs. These are difficulties indeed, but perhaps no greater than those facing the Scottish Board; and it is perhaps easier to explain the change as due to the inability of both men and officials of the two old coalfields of Northumberland and Durham, with their long traditions, to work together as one unit.

Early in 1952 a ninth headquarters department was added, a Carbonization Department 'to be responsible for the production of carbonized and other processed fuels.' The sale of these products remained the responsibility of the Marketing Department. The acquisition of carbonization plants from the old colliery companies was largely due to the insistence of the National Union of Mineworkers, which included the workers in these plants, although other coke ovens and the commercial and municipal gas undertakings are in the territory of two general unions. When the Area Gas Boards took over the gas industry in 1949, therefore, the production of almost a half of the country's 'hard coke,'[1] and about 8 per cent of town gas were in the hands of the Coal Board. Co-operation on production and sales has been by no means smooth, and the change probably arises out of these difficulties.

[1] Most of the rest is produced by the iron and steel industry.

(c) *Problems for the Future*

The 'centralization' of the Coal Board has continued to be a target for criticism, and schemes for 'decentralization' have been put forward—notably Colonel Lancaster's plan to break up the divisions and concentrate management on enlarged areas. 'Centralization' and 'decentralization' are, however, vague terms, and we prefer to discuss the main administrative problems of the industry by reference to three more specific problems: the size of unit, control by the National Board, and the use of experts.

Proposals for 'decentralization' must seek for the devolution of authority to a subordinate unit. Which unit should receive this grant of power? The area was an essential element in the Reid Report's scheme of reorganization, and it has usually been selected for this purpose. Because the Coal Board has found it necessary to interpose divisions to control the areas, the areas have been criticized as too small, and Colonel Lancaster suggested amalgamation to reduce them to about half the present number. The present areas, however, have had to make use of sub-areas and agents to maintain contact with their collieries; so that the areas may seem too large if seen through the eyes of a colliery manager.

Even within the present organization the original size of areas has not given complete satisfaction, and there has been some experiment. In Scotland, where pits are small, areas include a large number of pits, and the size of some areas has, therefore, been reduced.[1] In

[1] By a further reorganization in 1951, two more Scottish areas were divided into two. See *National Coal Board, Annual Report and Accounts*, 1951, H.M.S.O., pp. 100–101.

the East Midlands, however, South Derbyshire and Leicestershire have been grouped together as two sub-areas in one area. But these small changes have had no noticeable effect on the general pattern.

This problem of the right size of unit arises in all nationalized industries, and we shall return to it in Chapter III. The structure chosen for the Coal Board has, however, met a peculiar difficulty. The miners have reorganized their old Miners' Federation into a new National Union of Mineworkers, which nevertheless retains (with some area grouping) the old district organization once common to both miners and their employers. As a result some divisions have to deal with two or more district committees of the union, each of which has its own officials, its own working customs, and fairly wide autonomy. The wage structure of the industry, the complexity of which has been little affected by nationalization, still contains district differentials. These were frozen in 1943 when a national minimum was given by the Greene award.

The second problem is that of the Coal Board itself. It has been entrusted with wide responsibilities for the conduct of the industry and to fulfil them it must have power and knowledge. Its decisions might be based on a few 'objective' figures about collieries and divisions, such as changes in total output and output per man-shift; but far more than in any other industry, changes of this kind may be due to local circumstances. If this means that the Coal Board cannot rely on recorded facts, it must rely on human judgment, and in particular on the judgment of the men who report to it, and they in their turn on the judgment of their subordinates.

To interpret subjective judgments, and to have confidence that instructions are carried out when an 'objective' check on results is difficult, requires fairly intimate relationships between the men concerned. The 'span of control' argument then applies. If it must work by these means the Coal Board is almost powerless to deal with thirty or forty separate area boards. It may be that, despite its centralized form, it is already weak in relation to the divisions, because of the reliance it must place on them. Despite its formal authority, the National Board is dependent on the co-operation of the divisions and the areas, and it has not always found it easy to coax them to fall in with its wishes—for instance, to produce all the figures it wants in the form it wants, to take the interest in science which it feels to be desirable and to show it by appointing area scientists, or to develop training schemes. Even the devoted and unsparing efforts of Sir Arthur Street, which almost certainly hastened his death, could not overcome the difficulties of remote control.

Looked at from below, however, the effort to control detailed action, and to supervise personally, because of the lack of means to check results and of the need for close acquaintance with subordinates and their work, seems to be interference, and to restrict initiative. Hence the demand for decentralization.

Perhaps the greatest single problem of organization inside the coal industry is to find the way of making the best use of an unusually limited supply of first-rate men, to overcome the lack of 'knowledge and experience' emphasized by the Reid Report. The provision of specialists at area headquarters might have been expected to overcome the difficulty. Under the Coal

Board, however, a headquarters production department and eight (now nine) divisions have also had to be staffed. Divisional officers supervise the work of the areas, and so make considerable demands on the time of area officers, who thus have less time to spend in the collieries which they supervise. An area general manager may find difficulty in seeing each of his colliery managers more than two or three times a year. Besides this, most of the work done by the area and divisional experts must be paper work, which will have its effect at the coal-face only if instructions are properly carried out, and if advice is absorbed and followed. If most of the best men are given higher managerial or staff positions, and have to work through their weaker brethren, will the best results follow? Is it not possible that their instructions will be effectively cushioned from having any effect at the coal-face? Is it not possible that plans will lose touch with practical possibilities, both for lack of men capable of carrying them out, and because the planners are losing touch with the very varied conditions under which coal must be got, and for which their plans should be designed?

Engineering skills were not the only skills in short supply. Industrial relations in the industry were notoriously bad, and amongst the reasons for this was the lack of specialists in personnel management who now normally provide expert advice and assistance to the managements of large undertakings in other industries. The wartime control had built up national and regional labour departments, and under the Board these were extended and area labour departments added. Recruitment was mainly from amongst officials of the union. The reason for this was no doubt a desire to gain the confidence of the miners, but it was not an ideal choice for several reasons. Trade union officials have not had the kind of training which is usually thought essential for this kind of work, and experience in protecting workers' interests may not be the best introduction to working for management. Besides this, there are obvious difficulties for all concerned when ex-union officials present the management's case in negotiations over wages and conditions. The ex-union official resents the suggestion that he has 'crossed over,' for he may feel he is pursuing the same object, the welfare of the miners, in his new post; his former colleagues and the members of the union, for their part, resent that skill and knowledge acquired in presenting claims may now be used to support their rejection. The one-time union official 'knows all their dodges.' Finally, the union officers employed by the Board were not always well chosen.

Besides this, personnel management is not quite akin to other specialisms—accountancy, the law, scientific research, marketing, or even engineering. A manager may be a good manager without detailed knowledge or experience in any, or even in all of these, so long as he is well served by his staff; but he must be a leader of men, and cannot delegate this function to a personnel or labour department. This observation applies in all industries, but is particularly important in coal, for the colliery manager has statutory responsibilities for his colliery which cannot be devolved. There is no doubt that in many collieries the handling of men is unskilful. To find a good personnel manager for each pit would, however, be impossible; and even if enough could be found and installed, they might be resented by both manager and miners as 'interfering' and they could not take over the leadership of men themselves. Even a good area labour department is too remote to do more than help those—a minority—who are eager to be helped with advice in labour matters. To overcome this the Coal Board has attached labour officers to some of the sub-areas to give them closer contact with the pits, but this experiment does not seem to have met with great success. It is at least as difficult for headquarters labour departments as for planning departments to achieve satisfactory results through unsatisfactory managers; and this would remain true even of the most competently staffed labour department.

One of the difficulties has been a conflict between the production and labour departments in some parts of the organization. It is understandable that in any industry decisions based on technical considerations do not always square with those based on human considerations, and in an industry crying out for rapid technical development, with a history of bad relations and a very powerful trade union, conflict between the two interests is perhaps unavoidable. But the various compromises reached in particular instances have not necessarily been the better for lack of personal qualities and technical competence in the labour departments to match up to the mining engineers at area, divisional, and national headquarters.

If the conclusion is that great improvements must await a new generation of managers, hope must be tempered by the knowledge that under directed training schemes potential managers gain practical experience under existing managers, and there is a danger that bad practices may thus be perpetuated.

2. Electricity

(a) *The Growth of Organization*

There are now sixteen statutory public corporations in the electricity industry. The Act of 1947 established a British Electricity Authority and fourteen separate area boards; it also vested a number of undertakings in the North of Scotland Hydro-Electric Board, which had originally been established under an Act of 1943. For most purposes the North of Scotland Board is independent. The B.E.A., however, approves its construction schemes and handles national negotiations with the trade unions for the whole industry. On the other hand, the B.E.A. is bound to take any supplies the Board chooses to offer at a price determined under the provisions of the Act. For most purposes the Secretary of State for Scotland, and not the Minister of Fuel and Power, is the Minister responsible for the Board.

The area boards are directly responsible for distribution to consumers, whereas the B.E.A. has direct control over power stations and high-voltage transmission. The boards are appointed by the Minister (after consultation with the B.E.A.) but they are responsible to the B.E.A. for certain matters enumerated in the Act. Thus the B.E.A. controls the issue of stock, the use of and contributions to the Central Reserve Fund; it approves tariffs and capital expenditure; and it may give Area Boards such directions 'as appear to the Authority to be necessary or expedient for the purpose of co-ordinating the distribution of electricity and exercising a general control over the policy including the financial policy of the Boards.'

Apart from the powers vested in the B.E.A., formal provision for co-ordination is made in the Act by laying down that the Chairman of the North of Scotland Board shall be an *ex-officio* member of the B.E.A. and that four of the area board chairmen shall serve as members in rotation.

The Organizing Committee which had to commence arrangements for the take-over had little difficulty in defining boundaries of authority. Power stations feed into high-voltage transmission lines (normally rated at 132,000 volts or 66,000 volts). The transmission lines feed into transformers which convert power into lower voltages for distribution to consumers. These transformers are the boundary between the B.E.A. and the area boards.

The grid system of transmission lines was transferred from the old C.E.B. to the new B.E.A. The C.E.B. had exercised close control over the operation of the generating stations which supply the grid. For this purpose it had divided the county into seven control districts. Now, however, administrative control was added to operational control, and it was decided that administrative convenience would be served by splitting these 'control districts' into fourteen new divisions co-terminous with the area boards. The operational control system was retained, and only seven of these new divisions contain a regional control centre. In some divisions, again for administrative convenience, power stations were grouped under a group engineer; transmission staff were organized, as before, in 'sections.'

The main problem of organization was to bring the large number of distribution undertakings under the control of the new area boards. There existed 562 'authorized undertakers.' Apart from the Scottish Board, the C.E.B., and a few joint authorities and boards, about two-thirds of this number were local authority undertakings, and one-third private companies. They varied greatly in size, and a number of the private companies were grouped by holding companies. Owing, however, to the scattered nature of the holdings, little more than financial co-ordination was provided by this system. Many of the undertakers owned generating stations, but owing to the grid control system the difficulties of 'hiving off' to the B.E.A. were partly solved already. The private undertakings could be taken over complete without much difficulty, except for the few companies who also supplied gas and water. For this reason in electricity (and in gas) the companies were taken over, and not, as in coal, only certain assets. The separation of municipal undertakings from the local authorities was a more complicated task.

There was no obvious unit of organization in electricity distribution such as the power station in generation or the colliery in the coal industry. It was decided, therefore, to take advantage of the existing organization by establishing districts, which usually covered much the same area as the existing undertakings. The larger undertakings had to be split up into districts, but in these instances existing administrative sub-divisions were frequently used. Conversely, a number of districts were formed by amalgamating two or more small undertakings. Thus out of rather more than 550 independent undertakings in the territory of the area boards some 450 districts were formed.

The amount of rearrangement varied from area to area. The North-West Area reduced 76 undertakings to 35 districts. The North-East took over 25 undertakings, including the North-Eastern Electric Supply Company, and arranged them into 35 districts. In the South-East the change was from 50 undertakings to 45 districts. A number of districts, especially in the south, are further sub-divided into 'branches.'

On the average each area board was responsible for about 35 districts, the extremes being the Midlands with 50 and Mersey and North Wales with 18. The B.E.A. adopted the same view concerning the proper span of control as had the Coal Board, and resolved to group the districts into sub-areas under sub-area managers. Eighty-one sub-areas were formed, so that the average is just under six to each board. The extremes are 9 in the East Midlands and 4 in South Wales and in the Southern Area. There is also considerable variety in the number of districts in a sub-area, from 2 to 19. (These 19 are in North London, where much of the organization of the old North Metropolitan Company has been retained). Yorkshire groups 23 districts into 7 sub-areas, and the Midlands has 50 districts in the same number of sub-areas. The most obvious explanation for differences of this kind is the variation in the density of population and the location of industry. Arrangements suited to London or Birmingham would not be likely to fit rural areas.

The B.E.A. has four full-time members: the Chairman, Lord Citrine, who served for many years as Secretary of the Trades Union Congress, and had been one of the original members of the National Coal Board before he accepted this appointment; two Deputy

Chairmen, Sir Henry Self, a Civil Servant, whose special responsibility was administration, and Sir John Hacking, responsible for operations; and Mr. Bussey, who had been General Secretary of the Electrical Trades Union before his appointment, and was given charge of the Labour, Medical, and Welfare Departments. Besides four Area Board Chairmen and the Chairman of the Scottish Board, there are three other part-time members, each with experience in the industry. Apart from the rotation of area chairmen, there has been no change in the personnel of the Board.

The area boards each consist of a full-time Chairman and Deputy Chairman, and from five to seven part-time members, including the Chairman of the Consumers' Consultative Council. Divisions are in the charge of a divisional controller.

Within each area, sub-area managers report to the Board, but alternative forms of control have been laid down for the districts. In some districts a district manager has overall responsibility, with a district engineer and district commercial officer reporting to him; in others the district engineer and commercial officer are directly responsible to the sub-area headquarters.

The officer responsible for each transmission section within the division reports direct to divisional headquarters. As explained above, the station superintendents may report direct, or through a group engineer. The main reason for this provision is the very unequal distribution of power stations between divisions.

The arrangement of departments at the B.E.A.'s headquarters follows fairly closely that of the C.E.B.

A Secretary, Commercial Manager, Chief Accountant, and Chief Legal Adviser report to Sir Henry Self; a Chief Engineer and a Revenue Purchasing Officer to Sir John Hacking; and a Chief Labour Relations Officer, Chief Medical Officer, and Director of Training Safety and Welfare to Mr. Bussey. In addition, an Economics Department has been added to Sir Henry Self's responsibilities, and a Chief Contracts Officer has been appointed. The B.E.A. decided that it would be unwise to take over entirely the planning of its own generating stations and transmission lines. Amongst other reasons, it would have put out of business consultants with important export connections. But it felt that the size of its annual outlay demanded specialized control in the negotiation of contracts, and, therefore, appointed a Chief Contracts Officer who was to work closely with the Chief Engineer and to report to both Deputy Chairmen—an arrangement which has its difficulties.

The area boards are served by a Chief Engineer, Chief Commercial Officer, Chief Accountant, and Secretary, together with a Purchasing Officer. The same pattern is followed almost exactly at the sub-area. In the district there are only two departments—engineering and commercial.

Each Divisional Controller is assisted by four or five engineers. They are the Operation Engineer (Generation), the Transmission Engineer, the Generation Construction Engineer, the Technical Engineer (responsible for major equipment and for technical advice to stations), and, in the seven 'control' divisions, the System Operation Engineer.

The rationale of the whole organization is again

'Line and Staff,' but, as with the Coal Board, this requires analysis.

The position of the B.E.A. and its headquarters departments is, on paper, fairly clear. The B.E.A. is the line authority, with complete control over the divisions, and limited control over the area boards. The departments should act as staff to the B.E.A. and as consultants to its subordinates. Departmental co-ordination is assured by arrangements for departmental standing committees and conferences at various levels. The pattern is perhaps a little less complicated than that of the Coal Board, but there arise the same problems of relations between the various levels of management, and between line authorities and specialists. As in the Coal Board, there is rivalry between departments. There have been, for instance, differences between the administrative and engineering departments.[1]

Within the field of the B.E.A.'s direct control, divisional organization is less straightforward. Some of the officers reporting to the Divisional Controller are clearly line authorities; for instance, the Transmission Engineer, with direct responsibility for the transmission sections, or the System Operation Engineer; others—for instance, the Secretary and the Accountant—are certainly 'Staff.'

Within divisions the position of the group engineers is akin to that of the sub-area managers in the coal industry. Sir Henry Self has written:

'Where stations are grouped the Group Engineer has complete oversight of his stations and is required

[1] See H.C. Debates, 25th July, 1950, vol. 478, col. 329.

to deal with the full range of functions including engineering, expenditure, manpower, and liaison with parallel Sub-Areas of the Area Board. . . .'[1]

It is not always clear, however, whether his responsibility within this 'full range of functions' is for a separate unit, smaller, but of the same nature as the division itself, or whether he is an 'agent' of the Generation Operation Engineer who acts also as a convenient channel for co-ordinating instructions and information passed up and down between the stations and the other divisional departments.

The relationships between area board and sub-area manager, and between sub-area manager and district, are of the same kind as between the B.E.A. and its divisions, except where districts are of the 'double-headed' type; this arrangement is obviously a modification of the 'Line and Staff' principle.

A possible variation in area organization has been thus described by Sir Henry Self:

'One Board . . . has under consideration a plan that would substitute an alternative intermediate grouping on a functional basis in place of Sub-Areas. Briefly, this plan envisages that the Area Board Chief Officers would supervise all work of a specialized nature which does not require frequent local contacts, and would provide a consultant service to all district personnel. Between the districts and headquarters there would be a sort of third dimensional organization responsible directly to the Chief Officers at headquarters. This would consist of a series of "group units" for each

[1] *Problems of Decentralization in a Large-Scale Undertaking.* Sir Henry Self, British Institute of Management, 1951. p. 16.

of the functions of Engineering, Commercial, and Accountancy. The group units would be allied to one or more districts as a permanent role, but would be available to concentrate part or all of their energies on output in any district within the Area according to a major plan controlled from headquarters. The advantages of this proposal are claimed to be a greater flexibility of effort resulting in economies in staff and in supplies and stores which need not be tied to a pipeline. Each group of units would be set up in accordance with the needs of its own function, i.e. there might be six engineering units, but only four accountancy units.'[1]

(*b*) *Problems of Organization*

In order to understand the effect of this reorganization on the electricity industry, it is necessary to remember that the B.E.A. took over from two existing permanent national authorities, the C.E.B. and the Electricity Commissioners. The B.E.A.'s inheritance was thus very different from that of the Coal Board. Although there had been a Coal Board in existence, no one regarded this as more than an emergency measure, and the verdict of the Reid Report was that, if the industry was to be reorganized, there was need for 'an authority, endowed by Parliament with really effective powers' to ensure that reorganization was carried out and was generally accepted. If such an authority was to perform that task, it had first to be created. In the electricity industry, however, reorganization might be regarded as an extension of the powers of an existing authority, the C.E.B.

[1] Ibid., p. 30.

The C.E.B. had constructed the grid system of high-voltage transmission lines, and controlled its operation. It used that control, and its powers under the Act of 1926 which constituted it, to reorganize electricity generation.

'When the Central Electricity Board was set up ... there were 491 authorized generating stations in Great Britain, of which 277 were operated by local authorities and 214 by companies. As a result of the Board's policy of concentrating production at the most efficient stations, the total number had been reduced by 1938 to 171, of which 136 were selected stations and 35 non-selected stations. All these stations were interconnected and centrally controlled, with the result that only 30 stations ran for the full year and 14 of the most economical stations supplied 50 per cent of the electricity generated.'[1]

As has been explained earlier,[2] the Electricity Commissioners were not in the end granted the powers contained in the earlier drafts of the 1919 Act. The composition and staffing of the Commission, however, made it a body which could not be ignored, and it had some statutory authority. It had, for instance, the right to approve development schemes, particularly those of the C.E.B. (and much of the credit for the success of the grid system should go to the Commission), and from June, 1941, all proposals for increasing tariffs had to be submitted to it. The Commission also had the quasi-judicial function of hearing and settling disputes between the C.E.B. and the undertakers concerning the price at which the

[1] *The British Fuel and Power Industries*. P.E.P., 1947. p. 158.
[2] See p. 25.

Board bought and sold supplies. It remains true, however, that it was first and foremost an advisory body, and because it had to rely on persuasion, because it was elevated to the position of an arbitrator, and because it used its position wisely, it had attained a high regard both inside and outside the industry, and could often act as the industry's representative.

Given the powers over distribution granted to the B.E.A., which looked so much like the old C.E.B. 'writ large,' and given the disappearance of the Electricity Commissioners, it is not difficult to appreciate that a reorganization whose main purpose was to rationalize distribution—an aim supported by many of the distributors themselves—appeared to be a subjection of the whole industry to the C.E.B., with the main protective agency removed.

Those who saw the Act in this way were confirmed in their view by the actions of the Organizing Committee and the new Board. It has been shown that there is some substance in the claim that most senior jobs went to members of the C.E.B. staff and not to local authority or company men.[1] Even if there had been no jealousy of this kind, the chief officers of previously independent companies or of the undertakings of proud local authorities would have been likely to feel that their translation to sub-area or district posts was something of a demotion. Moreover, the organization of the new area boards was to a centrally-designed pattern. The concession of the double-headed district did little to

[1] See 'The Distribution of Power in the Nationalized Industries' by J. H. Smith and T. E. Chester, *British Journal of Sociology*, Vol. II, No. 4. December, 1951.

allay the feeling that a pattern was being imposed by the ghost of the C.E.B.

The labour relations of the industry also give an impression of centralization. A Joint Industrial Council for the Electricity Supply Industry had been established in 1919. For most of its life it had concerned itself with conditions of employment and with national wage advances, leaving the settlement of rates to its Regional Councils. Shortly before nationalization, however, the Council adopted national standard rates of pay (with a London differential). The effects of this change were still being absorbed in 1948, and nationalization was followed by an insistence on standard practices which removed most of the loopholes left for differential treatment or for local bargaining—by the concession of special rates of pay or by reclassifying jobs in a grade carrying a higher rate.

In electricity as in other nationalized industries, nationalization also brought national bargaining and national rates for clerical, administrative, and technical workers. Previously, except on the railways and in London Transport, bargaining for these workers had been local, where it existed at all.

Moreover, the central authority has tried to increase its control of labour matters by the national appointment of the regional officers concerned—for instance, the employers' secretaries of the Regional Joint Councils. By no means all the blame for centralization in this sphere can be laid at the door of the unions.

The trial and conviction in 1951 of the Chairman of the Yorkshire Area Board and some of his colleagues on charges connected with exceeding a building licence was another centralizing influence. After the outcry in the press—usually an opponent of centralization—it was only natural that all those with authority set out to devise fool-proof methods of ensuring that their subordinates could not get them into trouble with the law.

Although so far we have talked of the grip of the B.E.A. over the whole of the industry, much the same thing has gone on within the areas, as it was bound to do if area boards were to carry out their job of rationalizing and standardizing distribution. The task was complicated by the need to weld together in one unit ex-company and ex-municipal staff, between whom there had been a good deal of jealousy. Even here, however, it may well be that centralization has been overdone, and the suggestion that the sub-area should be done away with as a unified command[1] might be taken as confirmation of that. In fact, many sub-areas serve as little more than agencies for passing information to areas and instructions to the districts.

In so far as the arrangements of the B.E.A. rest on the span of control argument they can command less ready approval than those of the Coal Board. It is at least arguable that if the coal industry is to be controlled at all it can only be done by direct personal contacts through the line of command. But electricity supply is far more standardized in methods and equipment, is little affected by geological considerations—conditions, apart from the distribution of consumers, vary little between areas or from day to day—and measurement of most operations is relatively straightforward. It may indeed be true, as Sir Henry Self has said, that one of the most important tasks of the B.E.A. and the area

[1] See p. 76.

boards was to devise standard statistics and accounting methods and see that they were used; but it could be done, and a centralized managerial structure was not necessary to get it done. If standard methods of checking can tell higher management most of what it needs to know about subordinates, surely the span of control can be greatly increased.

One of the major changes introduced by the Act was the direct subordination of generation to the central authority. It is now fairly widely held that this may have been a mistake. There is no obvious justification for maintaining separate administrations in the co-terminous areas and divisions, and it is no secret that a good deal of friction arises over the separation; for instance, concerning salaries. The chief officers of the areas are rated higher than those of the divisions. If the C.E.B. could control generation and new construction (the location of which, owing to planning legislation, has become a major problem) when power stations were owned by separate undertakers, surely it could do so if their administration, and the administration of transmission sections, were entrusted to the area boards.

3. Gas

Before discussing the nationalization of the gas industry, two observations should be made about the nature of the industry. There are no technical grounds for national organization like the national grid in electricity or the inter-connected railway system in transport, nor has it a financial problem like that which faces the coal industry because of the extreme variation in production costs from coalfield to coalfield. Secondly, even within the areas established by the nationalization Act gas supply cannot be compared to the electricity industry with its neat division between production, transmission and distribution. It is true that gas production and gas distribution are separate operations, and that high-pressure mains may come between the two. But the time when the whole country's supply will come through regional grids is very far off, and in the meantime a division of functions of this kind may be possible and desirable in the larger undertakings, but it would not make sense in the smaller undertakings which supply villages and small towns rather than cities or urban conglomerations. One area —North Thames—is practically one single undertaking. The relative importance of large and small undertakings in the other areas varies considerably. These considerations had an important influence on the forms of organization established under nationalization. It was due to the first of them that the Act vested the acquired undertakings in area boards and laid upon them the duty of developing and maintaining 'an efficient, co-ordinated, and economical system of gas supply,' and gave only limited powers to the Gas Council, which consists of the Chairmen of the area boards with an independent Chairman and Deputy Chairman. No national organizing committee of the type used in coal or electricity was set up to plan the take-over and the new administration. The area boards—which consisted of a Chairman, a Deputy Chairman, and from five to seven members (several of them, including the Chairman of the Area Consumers' Consultative Council, part-timers)—had to do the work for themselves. Because of this, and because of the different nature of the industry in different parts of the country, there is a far wider variety of administrative arrangements in gas than in any other nationalized industry.

Consequently, our first concern must be with the structure and work of the area boards rather than with the Gas Council; and, since no single area can be taken as representative of the rest, space must be given to several of them.

Before turning to the area boards we must say a little about the structure of the industry which they took over. Despite the existence of London's Gas Light and Coke Company and other large undertakings, the industry included even more independent units before nationalization than did the electricity industry. There were in 1948 some 680 statutory undertakings, about two-fifths belonging to local authorities (mostly in the midlands, the north, and Scotland) and three-fifths in private ownership (mostly in the south of England). In addition there were about 300 small non-statutory companies. Many of the private undertakings were grouped by nine holding companies, but, as in electricity supply, little co-ordination could be achieved in this way owing to the scattered nature of the holdings. The largest of them, the United Kingdom Gas Company, controlled undertakings which now come within the territory of nine of the twelve area boards. Each of the twelve boards (apart from North Thames) took over some 50–100 statutory undertakings. The Scottish Board, for instance, inherited 64 local authority undertakings, 10 companies, and no less than 120 non-statutory undertakings.

Amongst the new area boards the North Thames Gas Board stands alone. Its area, which is compact and almost completely urban, is far smaller than that of any other board, whereas in number of employees and volume of production the North Thames Gas Board comes first. The Board is, in fact, the old Gas Light and Coke Company with a few small undertakings added, and its organization has followed fairly closely the pattern of the old undertaking. Because of the size of individual works and the interconnection of their supply systems, functional arrangements have seemed the most satisfactory. The chief officers of the Board include a Chief Engineer responsible for production and a Commercial Manager responsible for sales. The Controllers of By-Products, of Services (e.g. transport, surveying), of Research, of Stores, and of Staff, together with a Chief Accountant and a Public Relations Officer, provide the staff services. The Station Engineer of the great Beckton Works, and Group Engineers responsible for from three to six gas works elsewhere, report to the Chief Engineer, and District Managers report to the Commercial Manager. In the more remote undertakings previously separate from the Gas Light and Coke Company, chief officers have so far been left in charge of both production and sales.

In areas which include a number of large urban undertakings together with rural undertakings, it has been normal to arrange these undertakings into groups or divisions, and to divide functions *within* these divisions. A General Manager has overall responsibility for the division, and is assisted by an accountant and officers responsible for production and sales. (In some areas distribution is separated from production and has its own chief officers.) Local station engineers or district managers report to the chief officers.

In areas of this type emphasis may be placed on the divisions or on the boards themselves. The Eastern Gas Board, which has only a small central staff, operates through Committees for Manufacture and Distribution, Sales and Service, Accounts and Statistics, and Labour Relations and Welfare. In these committees the divisional officers concerned[1] sit with members or officers of the Area Board. The committees report to an Executive Committee, consisting of the Chairman and Deputy Chairman of the Board, the divisional General Managers, and the Board's Secretary and Accountant. This committee in its turn reports to the Board. The Board even has some of its specialist work done within the divisions. The largest division, Tottenham, which took over from the major undertaking in the area, provides the Board's statistical service.

The Northern Area is an example of the second variety, with the emphasis on the board. There the Chairman and Deputy Chairman of the Board meet the divisional Manager concerned, together with the Manager of an adjacent division to form a Management Committee for each division.

In contrast both to the urban North Thames Area and to the mixed areas, there is a third type of predominantly rural areas, which inherited the smallest and most widely scattered undertakings. In them even

[1] The Labour Relations Committee includes the divisional General Managers because (amongst other reasons) only one division has a separate Industrial Relations Officer.

functionally organized *divisions* were impracticable. Managers of individual undertakings continued to have overall responsibility for production, distribution, and sales. Thus the Scottish Area has been subdivided into five divisions, three of which are further divided into groups. Managers of individual undertakings have been appointed to act as divisional controllers and group managers. A similar arrangement has been made in the South-Western Area. In Wales local managers have been brought together in group committees, of which the first report of the Wales Gas Board says:[1]

'In general, the Group Committee themselves elected their Chairmen and Convenors. The Chairman, therefore, enjoys the greater authority of an acknowledged leader amongst his colleagues; the Convenor is the Committee's administrative officer and general secretary. . . .

'Group Committees are composed of all Managers in the Group District together with some senior officers of undertakings. Board Members, whole-time or part-time, regularly sit as members of Group Committees.'

The functions of these committees are to consider and express views on the reports of individual undertakings, to consider communications from headquarters, which should normally be passed on through the committee, and to consider the latest figures of results for undertakings within the group and comparable undertakings outside.

It may be expected that as plans for constructing new gas grids are carried out (and their desirability was one

[1] *Wales Gas Board Report and Accounts*, 1949–50. H.M.S.O. p. 10.

of the main reasons for nationalization), the opportunities for functional specialization at divisional or even area board level will grow, but, without unexpected technical developments, it is unlikely that rapid or great changes will occur.

Turning to the Gas Council, we note that it has the duty of advising the Minister on 'questions affecting the gas industry,' and of settling with him general research and training programmes. The responsibility for making arrangements with the unions for the settlement of wages and conditions of employment rests with it. Only the Council can issue Gas Stock, and it must provide a central guarantee fund and settle the amount of contributions. Apart from this the Gas Council can act on behalf of some or all of the areas with the consent of the boards concerned, and interfere in the affairs of a board which fails to meet its financial commitments.

It might be argued that the Gas Council's powers, if used to their limit, would give the Council a very large voice in the running of the area boards. Whether this is possible or not, in fact the Council has remained in the background. It has done little more than continue the services provided by the industry's old associations —the previous Gas Council, which did the work of a trade association, and the Gas Employers' Federation. Most of its research work and training is still carried on by Watson House in London, which passed over with the Gas Light and Coke Company to the North Thames Board. Collective bargaining has been to some extent standardized by the fixing of two national minimum labourers' rates (leaving the grading of undertakings to the areas), and by the development of collective bargaining for clerical, technical, and administrative grades. Regional joint councils, however, still settle all basic rates above the labourers' rates for different classes of manual workers, and the general effect of nationalization in centralizing labour matters seems to have been much less marked in gas than in other nationalized industries.

It can already be seen that the gas industry has not had to face many of the major difficulties of organization which confronted the Coal Board and the B.E.A. Nearly all the problems of gas have been regional and not national problems, and their solution has been made more easy by the freedom of each area board to vary its organization to suit its own structure.

On the other hand, it must be remembered that the new area boards are indeed large-scale organizations compared with the undertakings which they inherited (apart from the Gas Light and Coke Company). The proud undertakings of the Birmingham and Glasgow corporations have become divisions within areas, and the North-West and North-East Board include many local authority undertakings which, before nationalization, regarded themselves as large concerns. Most area boards, therefore, have their problems of dealing with jealousy between previously independent undertakings, of settling the correct span of control, and of fitting functional experts into the organization. To the members and officers of the Coal Board or the B.E.A. they may appear to be small-scale difficulties; but within the gas industry they are very real and important.

4. Fuel and Power Co-ordination

Unlike transport, the fuel and power group of industries has been provided with no special body responsible for co-ordination. The Minister of Fuel and Power has authority in each of the three industries which we have just discussed, and it is, therefore, from his department, or from voluntary co-operation between the boards, that co-ordination must come.

It will readily be admitted that there is no problem of co-ordination of such pressing urgency as in transport; but there are difficulties. Gas and electricity are dependent on coal supplies, and all three industries compete in industrial and domestic markets. The edge of competition in prices is blunted now by shortages and controls, but these may not be permanent.

As has been mentioned above,[1] both the Coal Board and the area gas boards are producers of gas, and their interests in prices and distribution are not identical. The prices of all the products of the gas boards must follow coal prices, and the boards have made complaints against the quality of fuel supplied to them and against the relative prices of different qualities which, they claim, penalize them.

The choice of equipment for installation in housing schemes may favour gas or electricity, and the gas industry has continued to protest, as it did before the war, that electricity receives preferential treatment.

The Coal Board is also a producer of electric power, mainly to supply colliery needs, but with some capacity available for public supply. Since much of the fuel used for this purpose is of such poor quality that it

[1] See p. 62.

would not be worth while to transport it from the pithead, the development of electricity supply from waste fuels at pithead power stations might be useful as one means of alleviating electricity shortages. But should development be the responsibility of the Coal Board or of the B.E.A.; and if the Coal Board insists on control, will it be sure of the interest of the B.E.A., which would be essential to the success of such a scheme?

The principles involved in these difficulties must be within the authority of the Minister of Fuel and Power, and since his power to give directions 'of a general character' extends over all these industries, it is he who must take decisions on matters in dispute between the boards if they are not to go by default. So far, however, the Minister seems to have left the boards to settle their differences as best they can.

5. Transport

(a) *The British Transport Commission*

The avowed objective of transport nationalization was the 'co-ordination' of transport. If this was to be achieved there had to be a national authority with powers over the whole industry. The separate boards of coal, electricity, and gas would not do; either a super-board must be established, or the Ministry of Transport would have to have far more specific duties and powers than had been granted to the Ministry of Fuel and Power by the Coal Industry Nationalization Act (and were to be repeated in the Electricity and Gas Acts). The first course was adopted, and the

Transport Act provided for a British Transport Commission whose 'general duty' it is 'to provide, or secure, or promote the provision of, an efficient, adequate, economical, and properly integrated system of public inland transport and port facilities in Great Britain for passengers and goods with due regard to safety of operation.'

At the same time it was clear that if the management of all sections of the transport industry was entrusted to the Commission it would be hopelessly overloaded with detailed work which would prevent the giving of any serious attention to its 'general duty.' Accordingly, the Act provided for the appointment by the Minister (after consultation with the Commission) of five Executives (the number could be, and has been, altered) who should manage the various sections of the industry under 'schemes of delegation' to be prepared by the Commission and approved by the Minister.

The whole of the transport industry has not been entrusted to the Commission.[1] Some exclusions were intended even in the original draft of the Bill and these were widened during its passage through Parliament. The four main line railway companies (including subsidiaries), canal undertakings, and London Transport were taken over. The railway subsidiaries gave the Commission more than a foothold in docks, road haulage, and road passenger transport. Certain other road haulage undertakings were to be compulsorily acquired, but short-distance haulage (carriage for no more than forty miles and within twenty-five miles of

[1] For a fuller account of the undertakings vested in the Commission see an article on the subject by J. L. Henderson in the *British Transport Review*, May, 1952.

the 'operating centre') and vehicles operated under 'C' licences (vehicles not operated for 'hire or reward') were excluded. The Commission was empowered to prepare area road passenger transport schemes, and schemes for harbours or groups of harbours, and these schemes might provide for the transfer of road passenger transport or harbour undertakings to the Commission, which would take effect if the schemes were approved. Although some road transport and harbour schemes have been considered, no scheme for road transport has yet been approved. Under Part I of the Act, however, the Commission might acquire undertakings by agreement, and in its first two years it added greatly to its road passenger undertakings by acquiring the Tillings Group and the Scottish Motor Traction Company, two of the three great combines in that section of the industry. Although the Commission holds up to 50 per cent of the shares in many of its undertakings, the third great combine, British Electric Traction, has declared its intention of holding out, and no agreement has been reached. Local authority undertakings and a host of small private operators remain outside the Commission's control.

Air Transport was already nationalized, and its corporations remained outside the Commission's control, and, indeed, responsible to a different Ministry. Shipping was also excluded, apart from craft owned by the railways; although there were clauses in the Act relating to working agreements concerning coastal shipping and a Coastal Shipping Advisory Committee. The railway-owned undertakings inherited by the Commission included several undertakings on the periphery of transport, such as Thomas Cook's Travel Agency.

By the arrangements of the Act operations are entrusted to subsidiary bodies, and the Commission's main concern is with policy-making and co-ordination. Co-ordination is achieved mainly through financial control. The Commission issues stock and submits charges schemes to the Transport Tribunal (which has inherited the functions of the Railway Rates Tribunal and certain other judicial and quasi-judicial bodies connected with transport); only the Commission can dispose of any part of the transport system acquired, and only the Commission has general borrowing powers. Apart from these powers in the Act the Commission has laid down that it shall have the final approval of any decision on new works or renewal involving expenditure of £50,000 or more, of the appointment of the higher officers of the Executives and of their salaries, of major national agreements with trade unions, and of dealings in land above a certain value. The chief financial officers of the Executives have to submit annual budgets and a variety of periodic financial and statistical returns to the Commission's Comptroller. The Commission may also undertake special investigations into the financial aspects of the work of any Executive.

In its work the Commission employs directly a small staff of about 200, divided between a financial department and a secretarial department. The latter includes, amongst others, officers responsible for staff, works and development, and traffic, but these activities are co-ordinated by the Commission mainly through its financial powers. In addition, the Commission provides certain common services through a Public Relations and Publicity Department (including a film section) which deals also with commercial advertising, and through its legal section.

The Commission also acts as a holding company for concerns like Cook's and for road passenger transport undertakings. Although Road Passenger Executive members may sit on the boards of wholly-owned or partly-owned undertakings, they do so as representatives of the stockholder—the Commission. Wholly-owned road passenger undertakings come under the Tillings Group or the newly-organized Scottish Group: but these groups continue to operate as separate undertakings, pending the introduction of area schemes.

The Chairman of the Commission is Lord Hurcomb, who had long experience at the Ministry of Transport. Its full-time members are Lord Rusholme, whose previous experience was in the Co-operative Wholesale Society; Mr. John Benstead, ex-General Secretary of the National Union of Railwaymen; and two senior executives of the old main line companies. There are also three part-time members, one of whom was chosen to represent Scottish opinion.

. . . . .

In describing the organization of the various Executives, it is perhaps best to deal with the smaller Executives first in order to clear the ground.

(*b*) *The Hotels Executive*

The management of 45 railway-owned hotels, of about 500 restaurant cars, and about 400 refreshment rooms was handed over to a separate Executive, which has the distinction of being the only Executive with a part-time Chairman, although it includes two full-time members. That a separate Executive was intended by the framers of the Act is made clear by the mention of it in the Act as one of those to be set up 'unless and until other provision is made by . . . order.' The intention was, presumably, to increase efficiency by specialization. Since, however, the restaurant cars and refreshment rooms are ancillary to railway passenger services and the restaurant cars were normally operated at a loss by the Companies as part of their passenger services, there was a good deal to be said against singling them out to be operated by a separate Executive, whose accounts would be separately published, so that it would be subject to pressure to reduce losses which arise almost inevitably from the work it has to do.

In fact, the conduct of the Executive since nationalization gives little ground for supposing that its services would not be just as well provided by a department of the railways reporting to a Chief Officer of the Railway Executive. They have been improved since the low ebb of the war years, but this was surely to be expected. No great economies could be achieved by returning them to the railways, but if there seems to be no gain from separation, logic is surely on the side of treating them as part of the railways. If there must be specialization, the hotels could be left alone under separate management.

(c) *The Road Passenger Executive*

In 1949 the Commission decided to limit the responsibility of the Road Transport Executive to road haulage, altering its title to suit, and to set up a Road

Passenger Executive. As has been explained, the main concern of the new Executive was to prepare area schemes for co-ordination, and not to control wholly- or partly-owned passenger undertakings; although its members might serve as delegate directors for the Commission, and they work closely with the Tillings Group Management Board in the same building.

Preliminary moves have been taken on three area schemes; the first in the North-East, of which details were published, and two more, in East Anglia and in the South-West, which did not progress beyond preliminary consultations. Such consultations, with the local authorities of the area concerned, and with private undertakings which may be affected, are obligatory under the Act. Moreover, if a scheme is embodied in an Order, objections may be made, and if these are not withdrawn, the Minister must hold a public local inquiry. The hostility of the B.E.T. companies[1]—the manager of its Northern Company organized opposition to the North-Eastern scheme—was hardly more outspoken than the criticism from the local authorities, of the Labour Councils of the North, as well as the Conservative Councils of East Anglia and the South-West. Their main objection was to an area board chosen entirely by London—they wanted panels of local nominees—and to the transfer of control of fares from the Regional Traffic Commissioners, who retain their powers over all undertakings until an order has been made, to the Commission and the Transport Tribunal. They argued that a comparison of London Transport fares with provincial fares showed them what they might have to expect under the Commission. In

[1] See p. 93.

the face of this hostility the Commission and the Ministry seem to have been afraid to proceed with schemes, knowing that they would have to run the gauntlet of a public inquiry. The return of a Conservative Government in the autumn of 1951 has made further schemes very unlikely for some time to come.

In fact, there seems to be little purpose in such schemes as far as co-ordination *between undertakings* is concerned, for the licensing powers of the Regional Commissioners have been used for many years to prevent 'wasteful' competition and to promote the integration of services, by means of through tickets and pooling arrangements.[1] If the schemes are intended to make co-ordination of rail and road passenger services administratively possible there may be more to be said for them, but it would be difficult to judge them until the nature of such co-ordination is made clear. If co-ordination was to be no more than an increase in road fares to subsidize the railways, local authority objections would become even louder.

In these circumstances, little can be said about the organization of the Road Passenger Executive. If area schemes are to be prepared, an expert body is needed to prepare them. If no more is to be heard of such schemes, and the control of road passenger transport is to remain with the Traffic Commissioners, there may be some value in keeping a group of full-time officers to act as delegates for the Commission as a shareholding body. Whether such a group should be called an Executive or not is unimportant. It would not be a parallel body to the other Executives of the Commission.

[1] See A. M. Milne, 'Passenger Road Transport and the Transport Act, 1947,' *Economic Journal*, June, 1951.

(*d*) *The Docks and Inland Waterways Executive*

The inland waterways acquired by the Commission (which included practically all canals except the Manchester Ship Canal), and the railway-owned docks, apart from 'packet ports' operated in conjunction with railway services, were entrusted to the Docks and Inland Waterways Executive. The Chairman of the Executive, Sir Reginald Hill, was a former Deputy Secretary of the Ministry of Transport. One of its full-time members was from the Port of London Authority, another was a canal manager, and a third had been a dockers' official in the Transport and General Workers' Union. There is now one part-time member.

The two concerns of the Executive are not so unrelated as to make their inclusion in one undertaking seem unreasonable, but they are clearly so distinct as to require a functional separation right up to the Executive. From it run two lines of command, one for inland waterways and one for docks, and it also provides common services from a Legal Department, a Financial Department, and the Secretary's Department, which includes a Staff Establishments Officer, an Information Officer, and a Purchasing Officer. Functional responsibilities are allocated to the members of the board; the part-time member advises on Scottish matters.

Waterways are divided territorially. England and Wales are divided into four divisions under Divisional Waterways Officers. In Scotland the Caledonian and Crinan Canals are separate units. The Divisional Officer is assisted by an Engineer, an Accountant, and a Traffic Manager. For traffic purposes the divisions are sub-divided into districts with District Traffic Managers. Most canal companies owned few craft. What they did own passed to the Executive, and this, supplemented by purchases, now amounts to about 20 per cent of the total craft operating on inland waterways.

The docks under the Executive's control provide about 30 per cent of the dock accommodation in the country, mainly in South Wales and on the North-East Coast, although there are also a number of small harbours on and near the Firth of Forth. Where possible they have been grouped, for instance, in South Wales, Scotland, on the Humber, and in the Hartlepools and Middlesbrough, under Chief Docks' Managers responsible to the Executive. The Docks and Marine Manager of Southampton Docks is responsible to the Railway Executive for marine matters (i.e. cross-Channel services) in the Southern Region as well as to the Docks and Inland Waterways Executive for the docks themselves. The groups are self-contained for accounting purposes, but a Chief Docks Engineer has general responsibilities for repair and maintenance.

The Executive has managed to get a good deal further with schemes for harbours and groups of harbours than has the Road Passenger Executive with its area scheme. Schemes have been prepared for harbours in the River Tees and the Hartlepools, in the Clyde Area, and for the Port of Aberdeen (which, because of its isolation, has been the subject of a separate scheme of its own). The first two schemes have been submitted to the Minister. They provide for management by a Harbour Board appointed by the Commission and responsible to it—not to the Executive. The relation between the Commission and the Harbour Board would be almost the same as between the Commission and one of its Executives.

The Docks and Inland Waterways Executive has also the duty, delegated by the Commission, of keeping the trade harbours of the country under review. It published its first general survey in 1951.

(*e*) *The London Transport Executive*

London Transport stands out amongst the Executives of the Transport Commission, and indeed amongst the sections of industry covered by the post-1945 nationalization Acts, as a senior settled institution. The London Passenger Transport Board came into existence in 1934, and even before that the bulk of the undertakings concerned had been brought together in Lord Ashfield's London Transport Combine. In 1934 continuity was marked by the appointment of Lord Ashfield and his chief assistant, Mr. Frank Pick, as Chairman and Deputy Chairman of the new Board. In 1948 continuity was even more marked when all the five full-time members of the new Executive were either members or senior officers of the old Board.

Changes in boundaries and functions were negligible. The most noticeable alteration was the change in status from Board to Executive. The London Transport Executive is subject to the authority of the Transport Commission just as are the other Executives, so that its borrowing powers are limited, and its proposals for major developments, or for changes in fares, and its budget, must be approved by the Commission. Under the Transport Act, 1947, the Minister of Transport has far wider powers over the Commission, and, therefore, over the Executive, than he had in the 1933 Act over the old Board, whose independence was wellnigh complete. It will readily be appreciated that from within London Transport it is easier to discover the disadvantages of the new arrangement than the benefits which flow from it.

The organization of London Transport did not have to be worked out in haste by an organizing committee. It took over an organization which had been built up in the middle 'thirties, and that building was rather an adaptation of existing structures than entirely new work. The only major change since 1948 has been the merging, within the Road Service Operating Department, of the Trams and Trolleybus section with the Central Bus section; and this change has nothing to do with the 1947 Act; it arose from the conversion of the South London tram services to oil buses which was planned in 1946 and has been completed in 1952.

The Executive, like all the other Executives of the Transport Commission, is functional. All the full-time members, including the Chairman, have departmental responsibilities. Below the Executive also London Transport is organized on functional lines. The departments of two of the Executive members—for Staff Welfare and for Finance—may well be classified as 'staff' services, but there is certainly not one single 'line' of command to be serviced. The main responsibility of the third member (excluding the Chairman), is for Civil, Signal, and Electrical Engineering, and of the fourth for Operations and for Mechanical

Engineering. Each of these departments is an independent line of command, running down from the board to a garage, an underground station, a workshop, a power station, or another local unit. The Chairman is responsible for another group of departments—secretarial, technical planning, research, public relations, and advertising—which we would again recognize as 'Staff.'

The Operating Department, which accounts for well over half of the total staff, is now divided into three sections—Central Bus (by far the largest), Country Bus and Coach (the smallest), and Railways, each under an operating manager. Within each department there are two or three divisions. On the road services, garages, which are the operating units, are grouped into districts within each division; on the railways the operating unit is the line, which is sub-divided for administrative purposes.

The large staff of the Mechanical Engineering Department is to be found partly in workshops and partly on service work within the garages, under the control of Divisional Engineers, or on the railways; Electrical Engineering is divided between generation and distribution; and so on.

The most important point to be made about this organization is that it cannot be compared with the Coal Board, the B.E.A., or even the Docks and Inland Waterways Executive, although its total staff is more than half as large as that of the whole electricity supply industry, and four times that of the Docks Executive. London Transport operates in a relatively small area compared with either of those undertakings, and, more important, its undertaking is, in fact, an integrated whole. Its bus and rail services are a single service for a single area in a sense that Birmingham and Manchester transport services could never be, however tightly the two were bound together in a single administrative unit. Not only are the finances of the sections interdependent, but also the timing and frequency of vehicles. For this reason functional organization is only good sense. The operating and engineering departments cannot be grouped in independent areas like those of the Coal Board. If the comparison is with the Coal Board, London Transport is an area, a very large area with a very large staff, but that is determined by the size and population of Greater London rather than by any internal decision of London Transport.

For this reason the span of control of departmental chiefs and their divisional and district officers cannot be regarded in quite the same way as in the coal industry. For these are not independent commands. They must be compared with workshops and departments within a factory rather than with separate factories owned by a single holding company. In financial terms, or in numbers of staff employed, the responsibility of these officers is great, but their functions are not widely different from departmental superintendents or foremen in a single factory.

To treat so large a unit in this way naturally brings its difficulties, but many of them are unavoidable, for a completely integrated concern *must* be centralized. Many of these difficulties have been minimized because London Transport has had time to get used to them, and to fit its personnel into its organization. It is interesting to note that some at least of London

Transport's senior officers take the view that many of the benefits of the changes of 1934 have only been reaped in the years since the war, particularly that of being able to get together a co-operative and suitable team of officers.

(*f*) *The Road Haulage Executive*

If London Transport was the organization in which the post-war Acts made the least alterations, the Road Haulage Executive was probably required to make the greatest changes, even greater than those carried out by the Coal Board; for in road haulage even more than in the coal industry undertakings were typically small and competition keen, sometimes perhaps savage.

Up to the end of 1950, 2,867 road haulage undertakings had been acquired. The total number of the Executive's vehicles was just under 40,000. Since a few of the acquired undertakings were large, it can be seen that the majority were very small, most of them tiny in numbers of staff compared with a relatively small colliery, and without any element of the complex organization required for a large undertaking.

Because of this the changes had to be greater. Collieries continued to operate as collieries in 1947; the superstructure alone was changed, and however profound the effect of this change on the collieries, they remained recognizable units. But in order to provide manageable units within their organization the Road Haulage Executive had to concentrate the 3,000 undertakings which came under their control in just over 1,000 depots and sub-depots.

Vesting day was of relatively little importance to the Executive because it took over as arrangements were made with individual units. Its heaviest year was the second of its existence when it took over more than 1,600 undertakings with more than 26,000 vehicles. Accordingly, the main consideration affecting its decision on the structure of its organizing was not, and could not be, 'What form of organization will best conduce to efficient operation?' but 'What form of organization will make the process of acquisition administratively possible?'

The Executive has now five full-time members including the Chairman, Major-General Russell. The latter is responsible for public relations, the secretarial and legal departments, and finance. Mr. Clay, formerly Assistant General Secretary of the Transport and General Workers' Union, is responsible for Staff and Welfare; Mr. Henderson, formerly Chairman of the Traffic Commissioners and Licensing Authority for Scotland, is responsible for Organization, Development, and Research; Mr. Cardwell, formerly of Thomas Tillings, for the Operating and Commercial Departments, and Mr. Sinclair for Engineering and Stores. There are two part-time members.

Nine Divisional Managers report to the Executive. One of the divisions, the Special Traffics (Pickford's) Division, deals nationally with what are known as 'excepted' traffics; the other eight are geographical divisions, which, at the end of 1950, were divided into 29 districts (three or four to a division), 225 groups (nearly eight to a district), and 871 depots and 157 subdepots (just over four to a group).

The group is the main unit of command for day-to-day operations and the district for commercial matters and financial control. The division serves as a link between the district and the Executive, and provides services to the districts and groups. At the division there are five departments—Secretarial, Operating and Commercial (traffic), Engineering, Staff, and Finance. Below the division there are hardly separate departments, only specialist assistants to managers. In general there is no serious problem of 'functional' organization.

Some moves have already been made towards dealing with long-term problems of organization. Vehicles of a particular type are being concentrated in particular groups within a division in order to aid maintenance. Some progress has been made towards 'balanced running' between districts by making arrangements where possible for inward-bound vehicles to return with outward-bound traffic. In all divisions except London each district deals with all types of traffic, but in London there has been an attempt to concentrate on particular types of traffic in particular districts.

The great changes under nationalization have had their effect on labour relations. Not only undertakings, but also the men who worked in them, have had to be integrated into the new organization. The laxity and informality of a small undertaking has had to be changed to the routine and standardization of a large concern. Until just before nationalization the machinery of collective bargaining had been primitive. A Wages Board had been established in 1938, and converted by an Act of 1948 into a Wages Council, of the type which had replaced the old Trade Boards in 1945. In January, 1946, the employers and the unions had agreed to set up a Joint Industrial Council to supplement statutory regulation. The Executive and the unions decided not to deal with the wages and conditions of the workers in acquired undertakings through these bodies, so that a complete procedure for conciliation had to be devised. Formal methods of encouraging consultation between management and men on matters of welfare and efficiency were quite new to the industry.

Whilst it was suffering from these sometimes desperate teething troubles, the Executive could not shelter behind a complete monopoly. Besides competition from the railways and over shorter distances from private hauliers, over 10,000 vehicles operate over long distance under permit from the Executive (although most of these cater for specialized traffics) and the 'C' licences provide a very serious rivalry. It is not altogether surprising that the Executive has made losses during this period.

For all these reasons judgment of the organization of the Executive must be even more tentative than of other sections of nationalized industry. It has the appearance of being highly centralized, but in no other way could the new organization have been united and held together in its first years. The signs of strain are, however, visible enough to give grounds for doubting whether its organization will prove to be the best means of providing a flexible and competitive service.

(g) *The Railway Executive*

Before the establishment of the Coal Board the railway companies were, if the Post Office is excepted, the largest industrial undertakings in the country. They had over twenty years from the amalgamations under the 1921 Act to suit their organization to their size. In this respect they may be classed with London Transport; but, unlike London Transport, the scale of organization has been increased by nationalization. Four vast undertakings have been made into one even vaster. Consequently, although the railways were already large-scale organizations with an appropriate hierarchic structure, nationalization has added one more tier.

Each of the companies had tried to break down its undertaking into more manageable sections by adopting a functional organization. The work and staff of the railways were divided amongst a number of departments—operating, commercial, mechanical, engineering, civil engineering, and so on. These departments were not 'staff' departments, but *operational* departments, each with its own line of command.

The territory of each company was divided into districts, but these districts cannot be compared to Coal Board areas, electricity sub-areas, or even to Road Haulage groups or divisions, for they were subdivisions *within each department.* Each department chose the boundaries of its own districts to suit its own requirements, and each type of district was made up of quite different types of unit—stations, goods yards, mechanical engineering works, sections of track for civil engineering, and so on. This naturally emphasized the functional characteristics of the organization. The members of the various departments got on with their own jobs within each department. A common view of general railway problems could only be attained from the apex of the whole system, where departments were co-terminous.

There were weighty reasons for adopting this extreme functional organization. In a heavily-populated industrial locality a manageable commercial district may be small in area, perhaps the area enclosed by a circle of a few miles' radius about the centre of Birmingham or Manchester, but such an area would be ridiculously small for an operating district, whose size ought to be determined by a consideration of track mileage and of the flow and density of traffic. So other departments also have their own criteria; the Motive Power Districts require an area which includes at least one main locomotive depot which can cope with major repairs. Civil Engineering Districts are related to track mileage and to the number of buildings, bridges, viaducts, and other structures requiring inspection and repair. Signals and Telecommunications Districts depend on the location of signal boxes and of the equipment of the railways' own telephone system. Estate and Rating Districts vary in size even more than other districts because of the extremely uneven distribution of railway property over the country.[1]

All these districts were managed by officers—District Operating Superintendents, District Commercial Superintendents, District Motive Power Superintendents, District Civil Engineers—directly responsible to superiors within their own department. In most instances these superiors were heads of departments who reported to a General Manager responsible to the board. The L.N.E.R., however, adopted a different arrangement. Its system was divided into three areas—Scottish, North-Eastern,

[1] The Railway Executive now owns some 52,000 houses and land to the value of about £1,000 million.

and Southern—with Area General Managers. Certain functions, such as engineering, were centralized under the control of headquarters departments, but the Area General Managers were directly responsible for estates, hotels, and police, and for the two major functions—commerce and operations. During the war a Central Traffic Office was set up at headquarters under an Assistant General Manager so that there should be someone to report for the L.N.E.R. as a whole to the Railway Executive Committee then established, and this arrangement might well have been retained but for nationalization. The Central Traffic Office was certainly not the equivalent of the headquarters departments of the other companies. The Area Managers retained overall responsibility for their areas, and those who knew the system would have described it as 'a federation'—as three separate units using common rolling stock.

Under the Railway Executive the country was divided up into six regions:[1] the Southern and Western were the old Southern Railway and the G.W.R.; the London Midland was the old L.M.S.R. in England and Wales; the Eastern and North-Eastern Regions were the Southern and North-Eastern Areas of the old L.N.E.R.; and the lines of the L.M.S.R. and L.N.E.R. in Scotland were brought together in the Scottish Region. The central departments of the companies—or of the L.N.E.R. areas—became the headquarters of the new regions. In addition, a Chief Regional Officer was appointed, with limited authority. He is certainly

[1] For a fuller account of the organization of British Railways under the Railway Executive, see 'The Organization of British Railways,' *Public Administration*, vol. xxx, Autumn, 1952.

not the equivalent of the General Manager of the old companies, nor even of the Area Managers of the L.N.E.R. The first Annual Report of the Transport Commission says of him that he

'reports direct to the Executive, is responsible for the general administration of the Region within the policy and general instructions of the Executive, and co-ordinates the activities of the regional departmental officers. The Chief Regional Officer is concerned in the appointment of regional officers; he has considerable authority for new works matters, and all recommendations for the larger schemes pass through him to the Executive. He supervises the arrangements for the issue and acceptance of tenders, subject to the submission of the larger items to the Executive.'

This amounts to little more than a grant of authority over establishments and labour and secretarial matters within the region, and of the right to sanction capital expenditures of up to £5,000 (originally £2,000). In practice this does not seem to be far from the mark. The regional departmental officers are responsible for the operational activities of their departments to the headquarters departments of the Executive. In short, the Railway Executive has taken over the structure of the old L.M.S.R. and modified it by interposing between the districts and the headquarters an intermediate stage which has not, however, the autonomy of the areas of the old L.N.E.R.

The result of this has been to make the main departments of the Executive as big, or almost as big, as the old companies, if measured by numbers employed. The Operating and Commercial Departments each employ some 200,000 workers, Mechanical Engineering about half that number, and Civil Engineering about 70,000. Each of these vast organizations has its own line of command, its own hierarchy of management within which all the difficulties of large-scale organization can be observed, even before its relations with other departments and the Executive itself are taken into account.

In one sense, however, headquarters themselves are more departmentalized than the old companies, for the Railway Executive itself is a functional body. All its full-time members are railway men except General Sir Daril Watson; all of them except for him and for one ex-trade union official, Mr. W. P. Allen, were managers or departmental chiefs in the old companies. There are three part-time members who have no departmental responsibilities. Each of the full-time members of the Executive has at least three Chief Officers to report to him. Four Chief Officers and six Executive Officers with separate responsibilities report to Mr. David Blee, who is the member for commercial matters, and six Chief Officers to Mr. J. C. L. Train, whose main concern is with Civil Engineering.

Up to now we have described the organization of the Railway Executive as though it was uniform throughout the country. This, however, is not true. There were a good many differences between the companies before nationalization, and only some of those have since been removed. For some departments the London Midland and Eastern Regions have divisions between the districts and headquarters, three in the first, and two, both in London, in the second. In the Southern Region operations and commerce are brought together in six 'Traffic' Divisions, which are the equivalent of districts elsewhere. In the new Scottish Region the Railway Executive has decided to follow a similar pattern and through amalgamation has produced four 'Traffic' Districts.

Elsewhere the functions of the commercial department were performed by separate goods and passenger departments with their own Districts, and the amalgamation of the two has not yet been completed. The administrative difficulties of district officers have been increased by the transfer to the new regions of responsibility for operating lines which previously belonged to other systems, the so-called 'penetrating' lines:[1]

'With regard, however, to *operating* arrangements over important lines with heavy flows of traffic, any change would involve heavy cost in altering control equipment and interference with train and traffic working based on long experience. Therefore, generally speaking, the existing operating arrangements for trains and traffic working will be preserved, including the existing operating and motive power districts, divisions, and regions. . . .

'Such lines will be termed "penetrating lines" and the operating and motive power officers will continue to exercise the same control over them as formerly, with the difference that the main principle will be applied to the extent that the departmental officer will report to the Chief Regional Officer of the new (or geographical) Region for those matters coming within the function of the Chief Regional Officer. For

[1] *A Step Forward—Revision of Railway Boundaries*, published by the Railway Executive.

example, in regard to staff matters (promotion, redundancy, negotiating machinery, etc.), staff employed on a penetrating line will be members of the new geographical districts.'

All this must not be taken to indicate that there has been almost no change within the regions since nationalization; the amalgamation of commercial activities has involved transfers of functions between commerce and operations; Motive Power has been raised everywhere to a full department. Signals and Telecommunications have been brought out of the Civil Engineering Department; and there have been several other transfers of functions between departments. The department of the Regional Mechanical Engineering Superintendent has been reduced in size and authority compared with that of the Chief Mechanical Engineer of the old companies by the concentration of rolling-stock design at the Railway Executive and by the splitting off of Carriage and Wagon Engineering and Road Motor Engineering under separate superintendents.

Another element must now be introduced to complicate the pattern further. We have so far spoken of the departments as though they were entirely separate lines of authority, leading down from the Executive to separate operational units in each department. This is a fairly accurate representation of the links between Executive and region, and between region and district, but not so accurate for the link between district and operational unit—for instance, the station. It is true that at a large station there will be a stationmaster responsible to the Operating Department, and a Passenger Agent, Goods Agent, and Parcels Agent all responsible to the Commercial Department. In a smaller station, however, the station-master may have to deal with all these matters, and has, therefore, responsibility to more than one department. Moreover, he and other unit managers are directly responsible to some regional officers, such as the Regional Accountant and the Regional Staff Officer. Because of the functional nature of the whole organization these regional officers work less as 'staff' advisers to the line of command than in most of the industries we have described, and more as line authorities within their own department. This is particularly true of the Staff Department, with the unfortunate result that staff and labour matters tend to be regarded as the concern of a specialist, rather than as one of the main duties of line managers, with, if need be, specialist advice.

. . . . .

When we try to look at railway organization as a whole, it is impossible to avoid the conclusion that it is too big. Elementary economics text books have for many years told their readers that there are economies of scale in division of labour, in managerial and technical specialization, in special terms from suppliers, and so on; but that there is a limit beyond which the difficulties of co-ordination and communication outweigh these advantages. Ideally, there is in any given situation an optimum size for undertakings within any industry. Has the change from four companies to the Railway Executive gone beyond the railway optimum, if, indeed, it had not already been passed? The Executive's problems in this respect are greater than those of the Coal Board, although this latter has an even larger number of employees, for there is no devolution of power on the railways to separate and distinct units with general responsibility for everything within their territory, like the Coal Board's divisions and areas. The railway departmental organization is far more closely knit.

It is easy for the railway user, perturbed by inquiry offices unable to supply accurate information about services outside their own region, displeased by grime and unattractive buildings, angered by unexplained delays, and dismayed by missed connections, to believe that there is something wrong with railway organization. This impression is not likely to be removed by listening to the conversations of railway workers in refreshment rooms, or travelling to their duties, or by talking to them. Most railway users would be ready to accept the explanation, in the absence of a better, that railway organization is on too vast a scale. If they cannot suggest a remedy that, after all, is not their job.

There are, however, other reasons for the shortcomings of the railways. All that has been said about their organization must be interpreted with the background of a declining industry in mind. From 1921 on, the companies and their staff were dominated by the failure to attract sufficient traffic to show satisfactory profits, and all that went with that failure—the inability to raise capital for development, hopes of promotion deferred, recruitment reduced, an ageing staff, capable men looking elsewhere for jobs. The recovery of the 'thirties brought less relief to the railways than to almost any other British industry, and 1937 and 1938 showed that the prospect was further decline. Then came the war years of unprecedented activity and profit due to petrol restrictions, the displacement of population and the re-routing of traffic; but it was not the recovery of improved organization and growing hopes of the future. It was a period of improvisation and reduced standards, of moving traffic somehow with a continually reduced staff, of development stopped and maintenance cut to the bone. It was the activity of a fever rather than the return of health.

After the end of the war the number of staff increased and deferred tasks began to be taken up; on the other hand, the private motorist returned, the population settled down at home once more, and the number of road haulage vehicles rose. Receipts declined and costs rose. The prospect was little better than it had been in 1938, unless nationalization was to make the difference. Nationalization brought no radical new developments like the Coal Board's sinking of new pits, introduction of new types of machinery, and transfer of mining activities from old areas to new in Scotland. Because of government limitations on capital expenditure, the Railway Executive has been able to do little more than keep pace with current maintenance and make good some of the backlog of the war years. The B.E.A.'s capital development programme has also suffered from government restrictions, but the effect of this has been to prevent supply catching up with expanding demand. Perhaps this is as aggravating, but certainly not so depressing, as the prevention of railway development which might be the means of holding existing customers who are turning to other means of transport.

If nationalization was to bring radical change, it could only be through the co-ordination of the railways with other forms of transport, which was one of the main duties of the British Transport Commission under the Transport Act.

(h) Progress towards Transport Co-ordination

The enthusiast for transport co-ordination has normally defined that term in words something like these: the carriage of each type of traffic and passenger by the most economical means. The sceptic has often said: 'That is all very pretty. But who is to say in each case which is the most economical means of transport and by what criteria would the judgment be determined?' Those who temper their enthusiasm with caution may have replied to this that of course there might well be a large number of borderline cases in which decision would be by no means easy, but, broadly speaking, railways are suited for long journeys, with heavy loads and infrequent stops, whereas road transport is flexible and suited for short journeys, small loads, frequent stops, and roundabout routes. Consequently, road haulage and bus services should be used for local and cross-country work, and to feed passengers and goods into main line stations and marshalling yards, whence they could be taken on longer journeys by rail.

No one has published any detailed calculations of the economies likely to result from 'complete' co-ordination, but the enthusiasts have been confident that these will be large enough to reverse the pre-war decline of the railways, and to allow substantial benefits for both railway worker (and other transport workers) and customer. The sceptics have suggested that transport co-ordination could amount to very little more than high-sounding camouflage for a policy of 'soaking' road transport to subsidize the railways. How have things turned out?

It is important to point out at the outset that, although it may be the duty of the Commission to 'so . . . exercise their powers . . . as to provide, or secure or promote the provision of an efficient, adequate, economical, and properly integrated system of public inland transport,' the scope of its authority is limited. The existence of private short-distance carriers, and still more of the 'C' licence holders, and the political barriers to the use of the Commission's powers over road passenger transport, mean that the integration which it can secure must be far from complete.

As far as co-ordination of passenger traffic is concerned, relatively little has been done. Up to the end of 1951, 983¼ route miles of passenger services had been withdrawn and 179 stations closed to passenger traffic by the Railway Executive. Where it was 'necessary and practicable,' compensatory additions have been made to road passenger services. These changes, as the Commission reports,[1] have been made in the face of considerable and organized local opposition, but they have not made a marked difference to the accounts of the Railway Executive or of the Commission.

It may well be that little has been done because there is relatively little to do. The great bulk of road passenger transport is concentrated on short-distance work within and around urban centres. Elsewhere many of

[1] Annual Report, 1950, p. 23.

its longer services are on cross-country routes in rural districts in which population is widely scattered. The Commission itself notes that in most instances in which railway services have been withdrawn 'traffic had already been captured by the road services.'[1] There are, of course, the long-distance coach services, but if these were withdrawn, or if fares were brought up to anything like the level of railway fares, the effect might be as much to reduce the volume of travel as to transfer passengers to the railways. As far as co-ordination between road service undertakings is concerned the powers of the Traffic Commissioners have already been used to considerable effect.

It is perhaps too early to discover what advantages freight service co-ordination has to offer, for the main concern of the Road Haulage Executive so far has been to build up its own organization; and this is a necessary preliminary to integration. Some moves towards integration have been made. Road haulage divisional and district boundaries have been revised to fit in more closely with the boundaries of Railway Commercial Districts. In East Anglia a common commercial service has been set up. An Area Freight Superintendent 'will induce traders to look to the combined resources of the two Executives; he will endeavour to use those resources to avoid wasteful duplication of services.'[2] Some railway freight services have been withdrawn (397¼ route miles up to the end of 1951) and replaced by road services. The Road Haulage Executive is providing maintenance for Railway Executive road vehicles in some parts of the country. But all these and other minor changes do

[1] Ibid., p. 24. [2] Ibid., p. 24.

not add up to an economy of major significance for the accounts of the Commission.

Beyond this the Commission has issued, in July, 1950, a 'Statement of Policy on the Integration of Freight Services by Road and Rail,'[1] indicating the kind of traffics for which each form of transport is thought suitable. This was supplemented later by a similar document for inland waterways. An important transfer of collection and delivery services from the railways to the Road Haulage Executive has been proposed, but has met with considerable trade union criticism over consequent alterations in working conditions and perhaps also in trade union demarcation lines.

One of the most important means for the direction of traffic to the form of transport best designed to carry it must be schemes of charges designed to attract traffic towards particular services. So far, however, most of the proposals for alterations in charges submitted to the Transport Tribunal have been designed rather to increase revenues in order to meet rising costs, either by flat-rate increases, or by differential alterations in charges *within* the sphere of an individual Executive. The only scheme which attempted more than this was put forward in 1950 to bring London Transport charges and those of the suburban services of the Railway Executive more into line. We are told that 'in view of the varying circumstances connected with passenger road transport it has been impracticable to prepare a passenger scheme covering both road and rail fares outside the London Area.' A scheme for

[1] Summarized on pp. 21–2 of the Annual Report of the Commission for 1950.

freight charges is still in preparation. In the past railway freight charges have been related to the value of the merchandise—'what the traffic will bear'—and road charges to the cost of transport. It has, therefore, been easy for road transport to 'cream off' the most valuable traffic from the railways, and to leave to them the carriage of articles which either failed to pay or only just paid their way. Since the proposed scheme is based on loading capability 'as the principal factor' it may, when put into operation, have considerable effect on the choice of traders between forms of transport.

So far, then, the main result of the particular form of nationalization chosen for the transport industry has been to provide a body to supervise the finances of the various Executives, and to allow the losses of one Executive to be balanced against the profits, if any, of others.

6. Civil Air Transport

The two Civil Airways Corporations—British Overseas Airways and British European Airways—are, apart from some Area Gas Boards, the pygmies of nationalization. This is, however, balanced to some extent by the vast territory which their operations have to cover. Even in these days of the telephone and of the rapid transport which the corporations themselves supply, there are difficulties in exercising control over long distances which may equal those of exercising control over large numbers of employees.

B.O.A.C. and B.E.A.C. stand out from the other nationalized industries in a number of other respects.

There is no co-ordinating body, not even a co-ordinating body with the limited powers of the Gas Council. Apart from their membership, along with the Charter Companies, of the National Joint Council in which they bargain and consult with trade union representatives, co-ordination must come either from agreed arrangements between them—for instance, for the provision of a radio service for pilots—or through the powers of the Minister of Civil Aviation. Besides powers of direction similar to those in other nationalization Acts, the Minister is responsible for the operation of airports in the United Kingdom, which are owned by the Crown, and provides a number of technical services for civil aviation. Many of the services of the corporations compete directly with those of foreign undertakings, and international bodies of which they are members exercise control over fares and standards of safety.

Civil aviation has been dependent on government subsidies almost from the beginning. The companies which began to undertake the business after the first world war were soon forced to suspend services because of heavy losses. The introduction of subsidies allowed operations to recommence, but when the Hambling Committee announced its opinion that competition was adding to costs and that the subsidy would be better spent on one undertaking,[1] the four main companies amalgamated to form British Imperial Airways in 1924. In 1935, five small private companies amalgamated to form British Airways Limited to operate internal and continental services. During the next year it was granted

[1] Cmd. 1811 of 1923.

a subsidy to assist its Scandinavian services, and Parliament was again subsidizing competing undertakings. Partly because of this, and partly because of other difficulties—departmental dislike of the 'independent' attitude of Imperial Airways, conflict over development, and certain internal troubles of the company which were aired in Parliament—the Cadman Committee was set up and reported[1] in 1938 in favour of closer co-operation between the two companies. In the event, Parliament decided on amalgamation through the British Overseas Airways Act (1939).[2] Meanwhile, companies operating within the United Kingdom had been brought under the control of a licensing authority.

During the war B.O.A.C.'s operations were determined by military and political requirements. It operated, in fact, as part of the Transport Command of the R.A.F., and services were supplied with little regard to cost. In 1945 the Coalition Government announced a scheme for post-war development, the 'Swinton Plan,'[3] in which it proposed to confine the operations of B.O.A.C. to the Commonwealth, the North Atlantic, and the Far East, to allow British Latin American Airways, a company already set up by a group of shipping companies, to develop services to and within Latin America, and to hand over responsibility for European services to a new private corporation in which the railways and short-sea shipping companies would be the main interests.

Soon after the 1945 election, the new Labour Government announced its acceptance of these demarcation lines between the three undertakings, but proposed that all three should be public corporations. Legislation

[1] Cmd. 5685 of 1938. [2] See p. 36. [3] Cmd. 6605 of 1945.

followed in 1946, establishing the new B.O.A.C., the B.E.A.C., and the British South-American Airways Corporation. The latter was merged with B.O.A.C. by a further Act in 1949, after the disappearance of a plane had led to the grounding of all its 'Tudor IV' aircraft.

After a number of experiments in forms of organization, including territorial organization, B.O.A.C. adopted its present form of functional organization in 1949. A reorganization of B.E.A.C., announced in 1951, imposes a functional superstructure on its existing territorial system.

B.O.A.C. has three full-time and seven part-time members. The Chairman, Sir Miles Thomas, has particular responsibility for commerce and administration, the Deputy Chairman for operations, and the other full-time member acts as adviser on international affairs. Under the board the main divisions are: Operations, Commercial, and Central Services. The Director of Operations is responsible for development and engineering maintenance, supplies and catering services, and for the four operating 'Lines.' Each 'Line' comprises twenty-odd aircraft and a staff of a thousand or more under the control of a Line Manager. The managers of the home and overseas stations are responsible to the Commercial Department, which is sub-divided into sections at headquarters. The Central Service Departments—the 'staff' departments—are under the charge of a Director of Medical Services, a Chief Personnel Officer, a Secretary and Legal Adviser, and a Financial Comptroller.

The new organization chart of the B.E.A.C. is equally complicated. Administrative Services and Finance are clearly the 'staff' departments; but there are new separate directors in charge of Commercial, Traffic, Flight Operations, Aircraft Movements, and Engineering Departments. For practical purposes, however, it seems likely that at least some of these departments will work so closely together that they will hardly amount to separate departments. Otherwise it is difficult to believe that there will be satisfactory results. The Traffic Director is responsible for the administration and operation of all the B.E.A.'s stations (except for maintenance at the three main U.K. stations, which are controlled direct by the Engineering Department), through the Regional Managers for the U.K. and Overseas Regions, and through Area Managers subordinate to them. The Regional and Area Managers are, however, also responsible to other departments, particularly to the Director of Flight Operations, who controls the flying staff, and to the Director of Movements.

The board of B.E.A.C. has seven members; all departmental directors report to two of these—the Chairman, Lord Douglas, and the Chief Executive. B.E.A.C. is thus the only one amongst the boards of nationalized industries to adopt the chairman and managing director system customary in private industry.

Air transport has always been and remains a 'glamorous' occupation, in which there is a danger that spectacular show may rank before humdrum efficiency. This tendency has been magnified by the rapid pace of development forced by rearmament and war. After 1945, plans were altogether too grandiose, in other countries as well as Britain. Calculations of demand were influenced by optimism concerning technical development, which had far outpaced civilian demand. Consequently, for two years after the war the corporations were full of brave schemes, overloaded with surplus capacity and surplus staff, and making very heavy losses over and above the substantial subsidies they received from Parliament. In June, 1948, Lord Pakenham replaced Lord Nathan as Minister of Civil Aviation and soon showed himself determined to push ahead with the retrenchment which had already begun. Since 1947 the staff of both corporations has been drastically reduced, whilst figures of capacity ton miles (the normal measure of output) have risen rapidly. Consequently, in both corporations productivity, measured in capacity ton miles per employee, rose by more than 150 per cent between 1947 and 1950.

These changes were accompanied by considerable changes in the membership of the boards (no novelty for B.O.A.C., in which turnover has been remarkably high since vesting day in 1940),[1] and by changes in the establishment of posts at different grades. Redundancy amongst manual grades was handled with considerable skill. The deferment of prospects of promotion has been all the more serious owing to the very low average age amongst the managerial staffs of the corporations. Higher posts are unlikely to fall vacant in any number for many years to come. After making his new appointments Lord Pakenham continued to take an active interest in the affairs of the corporations and a share in their work exceeding that of any other Minister responsible for public corporations, even of Mr. Gaitskell whilst at the Ministry of Fuel and Power.

[1] See *Nationalization in Practice.* John Longhurst. Temple Press, 1950.

And the consequence was a tendency to ministerial interference in details.

By 1952, however, there were signs that the corporations were settling down. The membership of the boards had not changed in three years, the decline in numbers of staff had levelled off, and financial results were showing great improvements.

7. Steel

The purpose for the insertion of a separate section on steel can only be to provide an opportunity to explain why very little can be said about the organization of the nationalized iron and steel industry. Under the Iron and Steel Act the securities of all the important companies with a considerable concern in the earlier stages of iron and steel making vested in the Iron and Steel Corporation on 25th February, 1951, which thus became a holding company with wide powers over the industry. Little use has been made of these powers. The companies continue to manage their affairs much as before. Co-ordination is provided by the various committees of the Iron and Steel Federation, to which belong all the 'public companies' and a considerable number of companies which remain in private ownership. Control over the industry has continued to come mainly through the Ministry of Supply, through powers over raw materials, prices, and so on granted to the Minister prior to, and independently of, the Iron and Steel Act. The corporation, with its small staff of some sixty members, and the threat of denationalization always close over its head, has not been able to get much of a grip on the industry. The main use of its powers which has received public attention has been a few changes in the composition of the boards of the public companies. Perhaps in its first months it regarded its main job as the acquisition of knowledge so that its powers could be used if the Labour Government won the next election. After the Conservative victory it could do little more than await liquidation.

In February, 1952, the first Chairman of the corporation, Mr. S. J. L. Hardie, resigned over a dispute with the Minister of Supply concerning a proposal to raise steel prices. During the exchange of correspondence and statements which followed, Mr. Hardie referred to proposals which he had made for 'decentralization' by the grouping of companies.[1] No details were published.

[1] See, for instance, *The Times*, Tuesday, 26th February, 1952.

Chapter III

AN ANALYSIS OF PROBLEMS OF ORGANIZATION

1. Clearing the Ground

We have tried to describe the organization of the nationalized industries with which we are concerned, and to indicate some of the major difficulties which have arisen in the process of building up the new organizations. This is a difficult enough task in itself, perhaps impossible to do well in the short space we have devoted to it; but it is simple compared with the task which we have now before us, of judging the merits of the various forms of organization and suggesting means by which they might be improved. By what standards are we to judge? Are there 'general principles of administration' which we can apply? Is business organization a matter for rational discussion, or a field where science must give way to flair and insight?

If we could claim that there was a general science of administration, and definite standards by which the success or shortcomings of nationalized industries could be measured, our task would be easy. We should measure the results of each industry's work, and where we found it to be sub-standard we could turn to our general principles to discover where the fault must lie. But we do not believe anything of the kind. There is no such general science; there are no such established standards. We do believe, however, that rational discussion of problems of organization is possible and useful. Our grounds for this can be briefly stated. There are some questions which can be settled to most people's satisfaction by evidence—for instance, whether more or less pits are in operation to-day than on 1st January, 1947, or which of two locomotives can pull a given load faster over a given length of straight, level track. There are other questions which rational argument and evidence—at least, the evidence at present at our disposal—cannot settle; for instance, whether or not nationalized industries would have been more successful if the boards had included direct representatives of the workers, or whether nationalization can ever give satisfaction within the framework of a capitalist economy. So that in the present state of human knowledge, the answers to these questions must depend on beliefs, on faith, and we have little confidence in our ability to change beliefs. Between these extremes, however, there are many questions concerning which some evidence is available which may be used to show that this or that is the probable answer. Whether we accept the evidence as sufficient or the argument as conclusive will depend to a considerable extent on our beliefs, but for all that the presentation of the case is not a total waste of time.

Consequently, we intend to discuss the forms of organization which have been chosen for the industries which have been nationalized since the war, and whether they could be improved. This presupposes standards of judgment, and the only criteria which we can even try to handle are impressions about the effect of forms of organization on those who work in the nationalized industries, and guesses about the probable effect upon them of changes in organization. We assume that there is a connection between their state of mind and 'efficiency' (measured in terms of quantities, qualities, and prices), without being able to demonstrate the existence of the connection, or to estimate values for it.

Because we cannot prove or disprove many of the beliefs held by those we have called the 'doctrinaires,' our concern is mainly with the 'pragmatic' approach. The 'pragmatists' advocated certain changes in the industries which have been nationalized, and in the end nationalization by means of public corporations was chosen as the best method of making those changes possible. Within these limits—nationalization and the public corporation—forms of organization were selected partly to suit the desired changes, partly to suit the views about large-scale administration held by those who planned the organizations, and partly because of the variety of pressures which are brought to bear on all political measures. Our case is that, although most of the expected changes are desirable, the forms of organization which have been chosen are not those most suited to bring them about. We therefore propose to examine what seem to us to have been the main factors influencing the choice of forms, and to try to demonstrate that these factors need not—and indeed should not—lead to the conclusions which were drawn from them at that time.

Of course, there were bound to be some mistakes in carrying out such vast economic and administrative changes. It is not easy to compare the results expected from a changed system with the actual results of an existing system; amongst those in favour of change there is an almost unavoidable tendency towards optimism. It may be easy to calculate that centralized purchasing will reduce the average cost of items purchased by at least 10 per cent. If total expenditure on replacement and new equipment is £10 million a year, it is only too easy to assume that the savings from central purchasing must be £1 million or more a year. There is, however, another calculation, much less straightforward than the first, which must be made. Transport costs may well go up if stores are centralized; time spent in filling up forms and other work connected with the distribution of stores to the operating units will certainly increase. The time and effort of local managers and their staff may well be spent in an energetic attempt to wangle rather more than their fair share of the stores available, and their claim may well deserve, or at least seem to deserve, special consideration.[1] It may become necessary to spend time pressing for an exceptionally large share in order to ensure that an exceptionally small share is not received. And allowance must also be made for the effect, perhaps unconscious, of frustration and annoyance when allocations fall short of expectations. It is clear that the sum cannot be done without considerable experience, and even then it will rest on a good many guesses; but when it is done it is possible that no saving at all results from centralized purchasing. It is still more likely that there will be a noticeable saving if a strictly limited class of 'major items' of equipment are bought and distributed by headquarters, and that the savings

[1] For an account of difficulties of this kind in aircraft production during the last war, see Ely Devons, *Planning in Practice*. Cambridge University Press, 1950.

from the central purchase of other items are negligible or even negative. It may not be possible to discover a standard divisor by which to reduce calculations of the benefits which will accrue from changes, such as is used to reduce to a probable figure the claims made by aircrews of the number of enemy aircraft shot down, and, after all, some changes are successful beyond the hopes of their sponsors; but caution will usually be justified.

Changes cannot be isolated, and they will have other effects besides those which were intended. Some of these accompanying effects are unforeseeable, but some are not. For instance, when the Reid Committee recommended the establishment of 'one compact and unified command of manageable size, with full responsibility . . . for the development of the area' in order to free development from the restrictions imposed by existing company boundaries, and to overcome the shortage of skilled technicians, by grouping them at area headquarters whence they could provide service for a number of pits, it should have been clear to the Committee that the change would have its effects on the status of most colliery managers. It is not easy to make quantitative calculations about the effects of a change in status, but some of its consequences might have been explored. Again, if a national authority is given sufficient powers to ensure that reorganization is carried out, it will be likely to use those powers to achieve other purposes besides those for which they were granted.

Sometimes changes may bring results quite different from those expected. For instance, more than one report argued that the establishment of larger units would create more responsible and well-paid posts to act as an incentive to management. Experience has not been long enough to show whether or not this will happen in the long run, but certainly one of the immediate results has been to create responsible posts which in some instances have had to be filled by men incapable of matching the responsibility.

It would be idle to argue whether mistakes of this kind could have been avoided or not. Perhaps it was inevitable in 1946–49 that organizations should have been designed rather to meet the needs of the years before the war than to serve post-war requirements. It should now be possible, however, to make use of the experience of the last few years; to design organizations which, even if they too fall short of expectations, will be nearer the mark than the first shots; and to see that if the method of nationalization is used again, the forms are more suited to the purpose. It is in the hope of showing how this may be done that we now turn to examine the considerations which have determined the forms of organization described in the last chapter.

2. The Size of Unit

In all large-scale business undertakings there are divisions and sub-divisions each of which may be considered a 'unit.' The nationalized industries are not exceptions to this rule. The national and regional boards and the Executives of the Transport Commission are all units; for many purposes they are single undertakings; for other purposes the Coal Board's areas, the sub-areas of the Area Electricity Boards, the divisions of the B.E.A., the divisions of some Gas

Boards, the divisions of the Road Haulage Executive, though perhaps not the railway regions, may be thought of as units; and there are also the 'natural' operational units, the colliery, the power station, the gas works, and the engineering works.

To simplify discussion, we assume that in each industry a number of *functions*—production, sales, maintenance, accounting, planning, and so on—must be performed, usually by different people, often by people grouped in different *departments*. Where all the functions carried on in a given area are brought under the control of a manager, or a board, we refer to his or their command as a *unit of over-all management*. Some functions, for example sales or planning, may be reserved for national or regional authorities; even where this is done, we refer to subordinate 'Line' authorities, so long as they are responsible for all but specific excepted functions, as over-all managerial bodies. The *operational unit* is the term we use for the colliery, electricity district, electricity generating station, gasworks, and so on. The manager of each of these units is perhaps best thought of as having over-all authority, since a considerable number of separate activities within the unit are carried on under his control. In other industries—on the railways, for instance—it is much less easy to say which is the operational unit; if the districts or, as we prefer, the units immediately subordinate to the districts, are regarded as the operational units, the railways' operational units cannot then be classed as over-all managerial bodies.

Proposals to group operating units or undertakings on technical grounds relate to *functions*. One planning staff may, for instance, be able to serve two factories as well as one, and it will therefore be more economical for two factories to come together for planning purposes; one accountant may be able to deal with three or four factories; it may require little expansion in the sales staff of one factory to produce a sales' organization capable of handling the business of six or more factories; and so on. It would be possible in this way to argue that there is an 'ideal' grouping for each of the functions which may exist in a particular industry, and it might well be that no two groupings would be of the same size. But although an organization in which operating units were grouped into twos for one purpose, fours for another, sixes, tens, twenties, and fifties for still further purposes, might have calculated the most effective size of group to a nicety, it would certainly have produced a quite unmanageable organization.

Proposals for industrial grouping, such as those contained in the reports summarized in Chapter I, stress the importance of a few functions in the industry concerned—the planning and control of development in coal, the load-factor in electricity distribution—and propose a new unit, much larger than most existing undertakings, as technically desirable for the exercise of those functions. They then argue, sometimes rather glibly, that other functions—finance, research, purchasing, sales—will also benefit from large-scale operation, so that the new unit should be a unit of *over-all management*.

The units suggested in this way for the nationalized industries were the areas (not divisions) of the Coal Board, and the area boards in gas and electricity. They have no parallel in transport, except perhaps in the permissive area schemes for road passenger transport and for harbours. London Transport was already in existence as a separate undertaking, and nationalization of road haulage and the railways was intended to produce nation-wide undertakings.

The arguments offered for grouping collieries, electricity distribution undertakings, and gas undertakings for the more adequate provision of *some* functions were powerful indeed. In mining the haphazard boundaries of the independent companies seriously hindered development, and the shortage of technicians added to the advantages of grouping for technical services. The smaller undertakings in electricity distribution and gas were often inefficient in many ways; gas grids could only be developed if undertakings were amalgamated. In all three industries smaller undertakings found difficulties in raising capital for development; and there were considerable advantages to be expected from standardization of equipment and stores, centralized purchasing, and so on.

Since the case for grouping many functions was so strong, it was difficult to resist the conclusion that grouping was also necessary for over-all management so that the functions could be performed within a viable organization. There was room for a good deal of argument about the exact size of the groupings, and in one or two industries the nationalizers chose areas of too ambitious a size. But at the moment we wish to call attention to an even more important matter.

The point we wish to emphasize is that a whole series of managerial levels cannot be justified by the argument for grouping functions. The Coal Board's divisions and sub-areas, electricity sub-areas, gas divisions, road haulage divisions, districts, and groups may be useful groupings for one function or for some functions, but this cannot justify their existence as units of over-all management—and all or almost all of the sub-divisions mentioned have over-all authority. The nationalizers accepted coal, gas, and electricity areas as the most suitable units for grouping for most functions and granted them authority over all functions to allow them scope to do the task expected of them. If it was afterwards discovered that different groupings were required for some of these other functions, it did not follow that their managements should also have over-all authority. The case for a series of managerial levels is quite distinct and rests on assumptions about proper span of managerial control. These assumptions, to which we have already referred on several occasions whilst describing the various organizations, require further examination, which we intend to provide in the Section on 'Centralization and Decentralization' below.

Furthermore, over-all management may have its own requirements and limitations, which should be considered in choosing areas for grouping. Indeed, theories about the span of control constitute a recognition of the truth of this statement. One of the most important tasks of over-all management is to deal with men, to cope with personnel problems. We would suggest that insufficient consideration was given to this in the construction of the organizations of the nationalized industries; to this point also we shall return.

3. The National Authority

The reports which we have so often quoted all argued that, since voluntary reorganization was not forthcoming in the industries with which they were concerned, compulsion would have to be applied by statute, if there was to be reorganization. They were not agreed on the way in which compulsion should be applied. The majority of the Royal Commission on Transport, indeed, thought co-ordination of transport by compulsion unnecessary, and would not commit itself to a final choice between a government department, a private combine, or a public corporation as the best means of doing the job if it had to be done. The McGowan Committee wanted 'definite and adequate compulsory powers' to be granted, presumably to the responsible Minister. The Reid Committee wanted similar powers to be granted to 'an Authority' which was to supervise (but not to own) the coal industry. The Heyworth Committee alone proposed regional boards to own and to manage the gas industry.

All the *national* bodies thus suggested—apart from the 'Additional Recommendations' of three members of the Royal Commission on Transport[1]—were not

[1] These members argued that 'all the available means of transport' should be 'placed under common management.' They pointed to the success of the B.B.C. and the various harbour authorities, and argued:

'It may be urged that the Trust which we propose is incomparably bigger than any existing public utility body and that therefore all precedents are fallacious and comparisons are misleading. On the other hand, if a system succeeds on a comparatively small scale, there is no reason why it should fail on a big scale. This is the age of big businesses. Throughout the world mammoth organizations are found concerned with the production and marketing of materials, with manufacture, distribution, and communications, which were looked upon as utopian thirty years ago.'

conceived as managerial bodies. They were to be government departments with only regulatory functions, or Commissions like the Electricity Commissioners (but with greater powers), whose task it would be to see that reorganization was carried out.

The Labour Party willingly accepted these proposals, and added considerably to them. They were convinced that a public corporation was the right body to carry out reorganization, and thought of the public corporation as a managerial body, since all the examples before them—the B.B.C., C.E.B., L.P.T.B., and so on—managed their undertakings. The Party was also firmly committed—the more so after the disaster of 1931 and the subsequent 'Keynesian revolution' in economic thought—to national planning. Accordingly, the powers granted to the new national boards to supervise reorganization and to carry on over-all management were to be supplemented by ministerial powers of direction to make sure that each nationalized industry could be made to comply with cabinet decisions concerning national economic policy. Furthermore, the Party had frequently argued that great economic power should be subjected to popular control. The grant of powers of direction to the Minister, who is constitutionally responsible to Parliament, would also satisfy this requirement.

Thus two national authorities, the boards and the Ministers, emerged in the post-1945 Acts. Between them these two authorities had to carry out at least four separate functions which the Labour Party had accepted from the reports, or added to them; namely, supervision of reorganization, national management, co-ordination with general economic policy, and provision of public accountability. It is hardly surprising that, as a result, some confusion has arisen; and we must now try to unravel the tangle.

The need for an authority to supervise and enforce reorganization was hardly disputable. There was too much evidence to show that voluntary action would not and could not bring results.

The need for national planning is almost as firmly established as the need for supervision. It is to-day a commonplace enough remark to point out that the political parties in Britain have no quarrel about whether the welfare state is desirable, high taxation inevitable, and economic planning and economic controls necessary. The most that they find to dispute is the fraction more or the fraction less.[1] If this is so there ought not to be much controversy about the ministerial powers of direction written into the nationalization Acts.[2]

If we go so far we have already admitted responsibility to Parliament. The Minister has powers and his use of them, or his failure to use them, may be questioned and debated. We may doubt whether the ordinary run of parliamentary question and debate is likely to effect a considerable improvement in the running of nationalized industry, but in the extreme case, when public opinion is actively aroused, parliamentary criticism may have great effect.

[1] This proposition is developed at length in 'Government and Industry,' a Report by P.E.P., 1952.

[2] In 1952 the Conservative Government forbade price alterations proposed by the Transport Commission (and approved by the Transport Tribunal) by means of these very powers. The Transport Bill presented to the Commons by the Conservative Government on 8th June, 1952, proposed no alteration in the power of the Minister to give directions to the Transport Commission.

It is important to note that we have met nothing so far that requires a national managerial board.[1] Only the Minister can provide responsibility to Parliament; only the Minister as a member of the government can be expected to give the priority to national needs over sectional industrial interests which national planning requires; and there seems to be little reason for supposing that he will not be able to supervise reorganization. A body such as the Electricity Commissioners with extended powers might do the job better than he could, but the Commissioners were not a managerial board. It is only when we come to the fourth function—national management—that the case for the board can be established. National management could be carried on by the Minister and his department as it is in the Post Office. But after the massive accumulation of evidence and opinion in favour of the public board during the inter-war years, it has come to be accepted that the board is the right instrument for this task, if the task has to be done; and the onus of proof would

[1] In the report of the Birchenough Committee on Electric Power Supply (Cmd. 93 of 1919), quoted in *Electricity Supply in Great Britain*, by Sir Henry Self and Elizabeth M. Watson, George Allen & Unwin, 1952, pp. 39–40, it was argued that: 'any comprehensive and efficient system for the development of electrical generation and main line transmission in the United Kingdom must be not only a national system, but a single unified system, under State regulation, in the financing of which the State would participate upon a large scale. In our opinion, the State would find it far easier to assist with capital or with credit, one consolidated enterprise than a number of separate Corporations or District Authorities, differing from each other in constitution and acting independently of each other. Similarly, in the case of a single body, the State would be better able to prescribe regulations, and to exercise effective control for the protection of the public against possible abuses of a monopoly.' There are strong *technical* arguments for national control of mains transmission. There is no reason, however, to suppose that the objectives mentioned here—administrative convenience and financial control—can only be attained under a unified national system.

rest on the man who would dispense with the board and propose some other managerial body.

But is national management necessary? Certainly not in the gas industry in which the Gas Council's powers are closely limited by statute[1] and will no doubt continue to be so unless one or more area boards fail to meet their financial obligations. What of coal, electricity, and transport? In each of these industries there are some functions beyond those normally exercised by employers' federations or trade associations which must be exercised nationally if nationalization is to give what was asked of it. Because of the disparity of costs from pit to pit and area to area, the whole financial resources of the coal industry must be pooled for collective bargaining if collective bargaining is to provide, as the miners insist it must, a reasonable national minimum wage. The electricity grid is a national grid and must be nationally controlled; but it does not inevitably follow that those who control it should administer power stations and have wide powers over distribution. If transport is to be integrated, the case for a national body to plan and to

[1] The existence of even these powers is contrary to the recommendations of the Heyworth Committee which declared itself against any national body at all. The reasons for neglecting their advice on this point were given by Mr. Gaitskell, then Minister for Fuel and Power, in the House of Commons on 10th February, 1948 (H.C. Debates, Vol. 446, Col. 228):

'But we do not go so far as the Heyworth Committee in having no national body at all. We believe that there must be a central body of some kind, but that it should be mainly advisory and federal in character, and we therefore propose to establish a Gas Council. . . . The function of that Council is to advise the Minister, and represent the industry as a whole. It will negotiate with trade unions, co-ordinate research, production, and training, and will be the long-term borrowing authority.'

control finance is powerful, and the technical considerations in railways and road haulage supported national grouping, from which it was an easy step to national over-all management. The same is true of the two Airways Corporations. The Iron and Steel Corporation has not yet used its powers as a holding company to make itself a managerial body, and it is at least uncertain that it ever will—or should.

If we accept the proposition that these functions, and perhaps some others, are national functions, does it follow that we must accept the national management board? The answer, of course, is 'No.' We do not have to accept it. If there is no function which must be exercised nationally, national management is folly; if all or most must be exercised nationally, national management is a necessity. If some, but by no means all, require national action, it becomes a matter of convenience. And if, as we propose to argue, the inevitable centralization of other functions, which over-all management would demand, is highly undesirable, the weight of convenience is against national management.

Some of the nationalizers supposed that the powers of the national board were only necessary in order that reorganization could be carried out. After that—say, in five or ten years—it would be possible for the board to devolve authority more and more upon subordinate bodies. They could point to the example of I.C.I. in which amalgamation and centralization was followed in a few years by a scheme for decentralization.[1] Their

[1] See the chapter by R. A. Lynex, 'Imperial Chemicals Industries Ltd.,' in *Large-Scale Organization*, ed. G. E. Milward. MacDonald & Evans, 1950.

mistake, however, was to forget the difference between public and private industry. The national boards have been given general responsibility for the conduct of their industries, and have been made answerable to the Minister. So long as the powers of the boards are thus defined by statute, any person or body with a complaint or a demand—a consumer, a trade union, an M.P., a private firm—will pursue it until satisfaction is obtained or until the highest seat of authority has been reached. When appealed to in this way the boards cannot deny responsibility. Consequently, they cannot put into practice a scheme of decentralization in the same way as a private undertaking like the I.C.I., even should they wish to do so.

Before we develop our case, it might be well to ask why national management seemed so inevitable to the nationalizers. Amongst the many reasons, one was the feeling of the Labour Party that half-measures had been tried in the inter-war years and had failed. Another was a curious confusion in socialist thought; many Socialists favoured increasing authority and yet feared authority. We must, they argued, set up a public authority to do this job; but what if it does not do it as it should? Then we must set up another authority to see that it does, and another authority to supervise the supervising authority, and so on. But if no authority can be trusted at all, let us be anarchists and have done with authority!

4. Departments and Specialist Services

So far in this chapter we have assumed that there is 'over-all management' and a number of separate departments dealing with separate 'functions,' as though all these functions were of the same kind. This assumption must now be dropped. The *genus* department includes quite distinct *species*.

Some organizations have a number of functional departments with executive powers, as do the railways or London Transport. As we have seen, such arrangements may be troublesome, as when railway operating and commercial districts cover very different areas, or when minor local troubles between departments have to be referred to the highest authorities for settlement, but they may be eminently reasonable arrangements, like the Central London Bus, Country Bus, and Railway Operating Departments of London Transport. In many organizations the separation of maintenance services and workshops as a separate department with its own line of command has proved a satisfactory arrangement. We have already suggested the establishment of a separate functional organization of the Coal Board to have sole responsibility for marketing,[1] on the same lines as the marketing organization of the I.C.I. Functional organization may be the best arrangement where the work of an undertaking falls into readily separable functions, complete in themselves, each requiring the employment of a considerable staff (such as London's bus services and underground railway services). Local operational units within each department can then get on with their work without constant interference. But where functions are closely interwoven, functional organization throughout a large-scale organization creates delay, confusion, and frustration.

[1] See p. 61.

These executive functional departments must be distinguished from administrative departments which provide the necessary 'Staff' or 'common' services for management at each level. Local managers may need nothing more than one or two clerks. Regional and divisional managers and regional and national boards require accountants, legal officers, publicity managers, as well as secretaries and typists. The need for these services in large-scale organizations is readily appreciable, and so long as the staff which provides them acts as staff and does not arrogate other functions, there is no reason why their existence need cause difficulties.

It is possible to separate out a third kind of department whose task it is to provide services for the operational units rather than for higher levels of management. A mechanical engineering department at national or regional headquarters, for instance, has not only to advise the board or the manager there, but also to provide assistance and advice direct to subordinate bodies. If the main task of a department is to provide consultancy services of this kind and relations with headquarters are accordingly loose, it should certainly be distinguished from other 'Staff' departments, and the area of work, the siting of offices, the choice of staff should be determined by the needs of the operational units and not by the convenience of headquarters. In the extreme case, a consultancy service could work without a headquarters at all.

The danger in departmental organization at higher levels of management is that departments may appear to the operating manager as a number of separate 'bosses'; and amongst the few rules of administration which can be said to be in any way established is the principle that each man should report to only one superior. Exceptional men may be able to work for two or three superiors without disaster, but a number larger than that should normally be avoided. As we have already suggested, the 'Line and Staff' organization does not necessarily remove the danger, for two reasons. Firstly, because it depends on a distinction between policy decisions which must travel through the 'Line' and other matters which need not, a distinction which is in many instances difficult to draw, and which even an arbitrary code of rules would not cover satisfactorily, unless the code was itself hopelessly unwieldy. Secondly, most undertakings, if not all, develop an informal organization which grows around the formal organization and modifies, perhaps even transforms, it. Those with experience of the army will know that sometimes—at least in wartime—the commanding officer of a unit is not the key man within the unit. A battalion might be run by its colonel, but it might also be run by its adjutant, regimental sergeant-major, orderly-room sergeant, or, indeed, by some power-hungry company commander, platoon officer, or orderly-room clerk. In the same way, several departmental officers with dominating personalities, or with the desire to dominate, can make nonsense of a 'Line and Staff' organization chart.

We have so far been concerned with the relation of departments to the executive, or 'Line' authorities, both at the level at which the department is located and at subordinate levels. The relationship between levels *within* departments may also give trouble. The Chief Officer for Finance, for Science, for Production, or for

Labour naturally keeps in close contact with his regional equivalents, and they in turn with the appropriate officers in the sub-divisions of the region. But if this close contact is misused as a means for passing down instructions and for sending up complaints against other departments or against 'Line' managers, the department can easily become a 'Line' on its own, and the whole organization a group of ill-co-ordinated executive departments—or, in the terse phrase used in the nationalized industries, 'all Staff and no Line.' Thus it may happen that an organization formally constructed on 'Line and Staff' principles ends up as quite as unmanageable as the worst and most complicated of functionally organized undertakings.[1]

A further difficulty of departmental organization is that an organization chart which provides for a number of levels of management and a number of departments at each level tends to lead to the working out of 'establishments,' and a demand for staff. The numbers required may seem very small compared with the total numbers employed in the whole organization. At the end of 1951 the Coal Board employed about 770,000 workers (including staff employed in ancillary undertakings) and of these 40,400 (just over 5 per cent) were 'non-industrial' workers—a term which includes 'colliery managers and under-managers, engineers, and specialists of all kinds, as well as clerical and administrative staff.' At the Coal Board's headquarters at Hobart House there were about 1,400 employees. Wild criti-

[1] For a fuller discussion of the difficulties of the relationship between specialists and 'Line' managers in nationalized industry, see Nos. 6 and 7 of the pamphlets of Nationalized Industry published by the Acton Society Trust, *The Extent of Centralization*, Parts I and II, 1951.

cisms concerning 'hosts of officials' may be deflated by statistics of this kind, but not entirely destroyed, for the demand to make departments up to establishment is a heavy demand, having regard to the scarcity of specialists with the qualifications and abilities for these responsible posts. Empty chairs, however, cry out to be filled; an organization below establishment is a worry to the tidy-minded administrator; consequently, one way or another vacancies are filled. The consequences of these proceedings are obvious. The best men in the operating units are—or should be—concentrated at the various headquarters. The dross is left behind and supplemented with rapidly elevated charge-hands and foremen, whose speedy promotion is in some cases a brilliant success; in others a dismal failure. But only some of the headquarters' vacancies can be filled in this way. A number of outsiders are brought in. If they are first-class men the resentment against them may die down; otherwise it may not. Still there may be many vacancies left; by some means these are also filled.

If this is not a travesty of the truth—and unfortunately it is not a gross exaggeration—the best paper organization is reduced to a mockery. To take an example: it is true that the majority of colliery managers could benefit from expert advice in labour matters. Theoretically, then, to provide Area Labour Officers was a progressive move. Its effect, however, depended on the quality of those appointed. In fact, few were first-rate. Many were ex-trade union officials, not always successful in their former job, and now often suspected by their late colleagues because they had 'gone over.' Moreover, they lacked the expert training or the wide knowledge and willingness to learn which can easily make up for lack of specialist training. In these circumstances the result is that labour relations deteriorate rather than improve, that the new organization is regarded as worse than the old, and that nationalization is branded as a failure on yet one more count.

5. Industrial Relations

Nationalization was to do great things for the workers in the industries concerned. It would be a cheap jibe to say that the nationalizers paid great attention to improved relations in industry in their propaganda both before and after vesting day, and gave little or no consideration to them when planning and building their organization; but the jibe would contain just enough truth to hurt.

Early socialists thought of nationalization as one of the most important means by which income could be redistributed to the advantage of the poor, by means of the elimination of profits. Although much redistribution has been effected by other means during the present century and particularly since 1939, and although the industries chosen for nationalization were not those in which large profits were made, the idea lingered on that nationalization would permit bold improvements in wages and working conditions. This hope was doomed to disappointment. The change from equity shares to gilt-edged securities, and the economies of rationalization were expected to provide considerable savings, part of which at least could be used to improve the lot of the worker. In fact, the savings were not sufficient to outweigh other changes arising in a period of rapidly rising prices and considerable economic adjustment—changes such as those which pushed workers in the rubber industry from near the bottom to near the top of the scale of earnings during the war period, or kept the earnings of workers in the vehicle industry at a steady and noticeable rate of increase during the period of the 1949–51 'wage-freeze.' Since nationalization some of the workers in the industries concerned have done better than the average, and some worse. Miners have maintained the great increase in earnings which they won during the war, and have also signed agreements giving them supplementary payments for industrial injuries, compensation for loss of work when collieries are closed, and a supplementary pensions scheme, besides the Five-Day Week Agreement, which, because of a subsequent agreement on an overtime Saturday shift, has had the effect of increasing earnings rather than reducing hours. These concessions, however, were but a continuation of the wartime improvements of the miners' position, and the other nationalized industries have not so much to show.

Most trade unions favour standardization of wages, which certainly makes the work of their officials more easy—one wage increase thereafter will apply uniformly over the whole country—and looks after the workers in the least profitable—and often least unionized—firms and areas who may otherwise provide a drag on collective bargaining. In many industries, however, standardization would require some pooling system or guarantee fund to ensure that the weakest members of the industry could meet their obligations. Nationalization gave the most effective guarantee possible, so that in this respect nationalization allowed important changes in the system of wage payment. But again it must be remembered that the introduction of standard rates was the speeding up of a trend rather than a radical change. Standard rates had long existed on the railways, and were introduced just before nationalization in the electricity industry.[1] In mining only minimum rates are fixed nationally—piece-rates must be fixed with an eye on local conditions of work—but nationalization has put national bargaining and national minima on a foundation much more secure than the temporary device of the wartime Coal Charges Account. In the gas industry nationalization was followed by a national agreement on labourers' rates. Rates for higher grades are settled within each area.[2]

Standardization has its bad side. It naturally increases the pressure towards centralization. Local problems must often be handed up for national settlement in case a local decision might be out of line with national standards. This is true not only of problems which are properly subjects of collective agreement, but also of the matters of welfare, training, and efficiency, on which the Acts directed the boards to consult with representatives of the workers. We have seen in Chapter I how the demands of the unions for 'a share in management' came to be a demand for consultative committees. The statutory obligation to consult was a second important victory which nationalization brought to the unions. In order to fulfil the obligation the boards have agreed with the unions to establish hierarchies of local, regional, and national 'consultative' or 'advisory' committees, or to extend

[1] See p. 80. [2] See p. 88.

the functions of bargaining bodies to charge them with the duty of advising on these additional subjects.[1]

Two separate purposes—the desire to exercise greater control over employers and managers whom workers and unions cannot trust, and the desire to give the industrial worker a fuller life by granting to him the right to share in decisions which affect his working life—were often confused in the propaganda of industrial democrats. The distinction is of great importance in considering the work of consultative committees. Centralization is the obvious means to make the control of trade union executive committees and officers effective; but it takes decisions further away from the rank and file union members, who may feel that nationalization has reduced their share in management decisions rather than increased it. Before, they could see their own manager and get a decision straight away (true enough, as the trade union official would say, the decision was far too often 'No'); now they may have to wait for weeks or months whilst 'the machinery' is used. When the question at issue really is one of national policy the procedure is clearly defensible; when it is one of the small matters which continually crop up, and which make such a great difference to industrial relations—short tasks, for instance, which may be finished long before 'the machinery' has had time to give an answer—delay is far less defensible, and far more irksome.

We do not wish here to tarry long over the problem of labour relations in nationalized industry and the effects of the organization of the nationalized industries

[1] See *The Framework of Joint Consultation*, No. 10 in the 'Nationalized Industry' series, by the Acton Society Trust, 1952.

upon them. One of us has tried to develop this theme at length elsewhere.[1] Here we wish to stress only two points.

First of all, to give the worker a tolerable organization—leaving perfection on one side—he needs someone within reach who can be thought of as a 'boss,' who has the power to take decisions. The electricity worker who used to work in a middling-sized local authority undertaking was not far removed from the engineer-in-charge. Now, in a 'double-headed' organization,[2] the district engineer may appear to be no 'boss' because he must often refer decisions upwards. Perhaps the sub-area engineer is now the boss? He certainly gives directions to the district engineer, but he is at hand only for short periods of time. He has his own office and other sub-areas to attend to. As for the area board, some of its members may have been amongst the visitors who are often shown round, but since they are not introduced, it remains anonymous. Arrangements of this kind, and they can be paralleled in most nationalized industries, naturally give rise to epithets like 'soulless organizations.' If nationalization makes them inevitable, so much the worse for nationalization.

Industrial democrats might deny that a 'boss' could be the solution to the human problem of industry. So long, however, as we accept an authoritative system of management for industry—as both the unions and the Labour Party do—there must be 'bosses,' and it is of great importance that they should be in the right place and provided with the powers necessary to do an effective job. Even under a national guild or under

[1] *Industrial Democracy and Nationalization.* H. A. Clegg. Basil Blackwell, 1951. [2] See p. 73.

joint control—whether they would be satisfactory forms of industrial organization or not—troubles very similar to that which we have just described would arise unless attention was paid to separating out the functions of the various managerial bodies and granting sufficient powers to the local units to allow them to take decisions for themselves. The problems of large-scale organization cannot be spirited away by the device of electing managements.

The second point we wish to emphasize is that the selection of managers, particularly of those who control operational units, for their ability to handle men—and their ability to handle men in the conditions of post-war Britain—is of first order importance. Indeed, there is little sense in putting forward a scheme for reorganizing nationalized industry unless it can be shown that men can be found to make it work. And this is a matter to which we must return in the next chapter.

6. Centralization and Decentralization

Critics of the nationalized industry have already drawn attention to many of the difficulties described in the preceding sections of this chapter. The critics have also proposed a remedy—decentralization; that is, the devolution of power from a higher authority to a lower authority. Most of the schemes they put forward suggest the transfer of powers from a national to a regional authority, or, in the extreme case, the abolition of the Coal Board and divisional boards in favour of thirty or forty area boards, or the transfer of authority from the B.E.A. to the area boards in the electricity industry. Such changes would not of themselves remove the kind of administrative arrangements which we described at the end of our last section. They would not give a tangible local 'boss.'

We would prefer to avoid the word 'decentralization,' and to approach the problem from a different angle. All the reports which so strongly affected the choice of forms of organization in the nationalized industries were powerful advocates of certain measures of centralization, and other measures of centralization were desired by other groups of nationalizers—for instance, standardization of wages by the trade unions. Most Labour Party politicians were anxious to increase parliamentary and public control over nationalized industries, both by increasing the scope of ministerial control and, therefore, of parliamentary question and debate, or by setting up Consumers' Councils to advise the boards, to consider complaints, and, if need be, to ask the Minister to make use of his powers. Public accountability is a strong centralizing force, since in order to answer questions and to investigate complaints, inquiries must be made into details of administration. Routine checks and returns may be multiplied to forestall questions; and the result may be that most managers and officials acquire the habit of looking over their shoulders as they work. There is and has long been controversy over the strength of this centralizing influence, and over the balance of its good and evil effects, but no one doubts that it does exert *some* pressure towards centralization. Nationalization was thus largely a matter of centralization. Public ownership was necessary in order to allow some functions to be centralized. Accordingly, the first question to be asked is not: which of the now centralized powers can be devolved? It is rather: what functions had to be centralized, and must remain centralized, in order to achieve the aims of nationalization?

We must admit that this is a radically different approach from that of the nationalization Acts. The Acts established national bodies, or, at the most, national and regional bodies responsible to Parliament with general powers over the assets or undertakings acquired, and left it to them to make arrangements for devolving responsibility to subordinate authorities of their own choosing. The inevitable result was the choice of organization which looked from the top to be the most convenient, to give a manageable span of control and little attention was paid to the aspect which the pyramid of control presented to those at or near the base.

The nationalizers might have gone about their task in a different way. They might have asked what changes they wished to see in the nationalized industry: they might then have considered where authority must be located and how much authority must be granted to bring those changes about; after that they might have proceeded to provide by statute for the establishment of the required bodies and for the grant of the required powers. The bodies then set up could have been held accountable to the Minister and to Parliament for those matters in which they were given specific responsibilities. Thus they would not have been granted wide and general responsibility beyond the powers of human beings to fulfil, which they would nevertheless have to try to fulfil so long as they were held accountable.

To put the argument in a more concrete form. In coal, gas, and electricity there was need for new authorities which would plan development over wide areas, reorganize the varied undertakings within those areas, and provide certain common services which the separate undertakings could not satisfactorily provide for themselves. To accomplish this, regional or area boards might have been set up with responsibility for planning and for financial control—that is, to carry out duties closely akin to those of a holding company. There would have also been need for a national authority to see that the new boards did in fact fulfil their duties, and to take such decisions as the general economic plans of the government might require. These functions do not require a national board, certainly not a national *managerial* board, and the nationalizers might well have seen fit to leave them to the Minister. In exercising them he would have been held responsible to Parliament, and, because his authority was defined, the boundaries between parliamentary control and administrative detail would have been more clearly visible than they now are. As it is, the responsibilities of Ministers and boards overlap. The Minister is not responsible for matters of administration, but any 'general policy' decisions taken by the boards come also within the sphere of his authority. Accordingly, no one without special information knows to whom is due praise for successes or blame for failures. It is wasteful for the Ministry to duplicate the staff of the board; but if there is no duplication how is the Minister to know whether or not he is fulfilling his responsibilities wisely? These difficulties might have been avoided if the responsibility for major national decisions had been given to the Minister, and to him alone. The Minister might have been able to use his powers more wisely if, in addition, he had been assisted by the advice of a small commission, without managerial responsibilities, following the pattern of the Electricity Commission.

The nationalizers could have gone about their business in this way, and it would still be possible to follow it in working out schemes of reorganization for the nationalized industries; to make of the operational units the only bodies in those industries with over-all responsibilities, and to limit the authority of such regional or national bodies as may be necessary to those functions which must be centrally exercised, and which they can reasonably be expected to perform. Of course, it would be impossible to proceed as though the nationalization Acts had not been passed, as though the new hierarchies of managerial bodies had not been established; plans for reorganization would have to take them into account. And it would be foolish to act hastily and to attempt too many changes at once; for the results of violent reorganization may be quite as bad as the results of poor organization.

Enough has been said to arouse a storm of criticism. How would these proposals affect transport? What would happen to electricity generation and transmission? How would the miners' national minimum wage be supported? Are not the nationalized industries so different that no one scheme could be applied to them all? The relevance of these questions, and a host of others, must be recognized, and they cannot be answered in a few words. We have devoted our next, and last, chapter to giving our answers to them, and to showing how the methods of organization we have just outlined might be applied to each of the nationalized industries.

Before we turn to this task, however, we wish to meet some general objections which could be made against this or any other scheme of reorganization. 'You have already allowed,' the critic might say, 'that informal organization may modify and even transform formal organization. If you set up regional and national bodies of this modified variety, what is to prevent them from taking to themselves, through financial control, powers of direction, and so on, all the authority which you propose to strip from the existing bodies?'

Our reply is twofold. First of all, formal organization affects informal organization just as the latter modifies the former. Informal organization will develop, but in the federal forms we have just outlined it is likely to be of a very different kind from the informal organization of our present unitary systems. Secondly, this kind of informal organization is affected almost as much by the number of levels of authority as by the powers allotted to each authority. If two or three levels of authority are established, and each is given wide responsibilities, they cannot avoid drawing power to themselves. They must justify their existence, they must collect their own returns, they must take decisions, and the powers which they absorb in the process must come from below, just as superior bodies feed upon them. If our proposals were followed, the number of levels of authority would be reduced. There would be no need for divisions *and* areas in coal, for areas *and* sub-areas in electricity, and there would be no need for both a Minister and a national board. This, we suggest, together with the revision of the powers and duties of the authorities which remain, would so change the shape of the organization that informal pressures would be hard put to it to make it the same as before. Indeed, informal pressures might as well work with these changes as against them.

The critic may put his objection in another form. 'Good administrative methods cannot be laid down by statute,' he may say. 'They depend on the formation of good habits within the nationalized industries. The new administrations are just beginning to settle down. By far the best thing is to leave them alone and let the process continue.'

It must at once be admitted that good administration does depend on good habits, and Parliament cannot lay down habits by legislation. But some organizations are so constructed that good habits are discouraged and bad habits develop without restraint. Parliament can make rules, and all we ask is that Parliament should lay down a clear and reasonable set of rules for each nationalized industry, a set of rules which would support good habits as they grew to strength and maturity.

Chapter IV

THE REORGANIZATION OF NATIONALIZED INDUSTRY

1. Some Disclaimers

Before coming to detailed proposals for changes in the organization of the nationalized industries, we should like to go some way towards defining those proposals negatively by stating explicitly what they do not include, and what they cannot accomplish.

First of all, they are not proposals for de-nationalization. Nationalization is a matter of ownership, of public ownership through acquisition by Parliament, as opposed to public ownership by local authorities. By 1945 it had become abundantly clear that nationalization was the essential prerequisite of reorganization in the industries which have been nationalized; or, at the very least, if other methods, such as compulsory amalgamation in a private monopoly, could have brought some improvements, that nationalization was the best amongst the various methods available, and the only one which would allow all the desirable changes to be made: reorganization was essential, nationalization the prerequisite. Our difference with those we have called 'the nationalizers' is over some of the measures of reorganization which they adopted. They thought that nationalization entailed national management. *We think that nationalization is compatible with small-scale operation.* Not only do we think the two are compatible; we would go further, and assert that unless means can be found to reorganize our basic industries and subject them to public control without subjecting them to national management, one of the greatest economic problems of twentieth-century Britain must go unsolved.

Secondly, our proposals do not imply the 'de-nationalization of wages.' Whether or not it is desirable, national wage negotiations have become general in British industry. More than that, some industries, both private and nationalized, have come (through the process of settling national advances on locally fixed rates, or of settling national minimum rates) to the settlement of standard national rates. A single national undertaking is by no means necessary to national negotiations, or to standard national rates. Employers' federations can conduct national negotiations, and some employers' federations have agreed standard rates. One of the industries with greatest variation in the size of undertaking, the building industry, agrees standard rates. It allows slight variations between area and area, but even these must receive national sanction.[1] The local authorities, whose capacity to pay certainly varies, also pay standard rates with even fewer variations. Would not the association of fifteen, twenty, or even thirty nationally-owned regional boards be able to do the same? There are, admittedly, exceptional cases, in which the variation in capacity to pay is too great, too great even to allow a reasonable national minimum wage, and the mining industry is

[1] It must be admitted that, since the war, many building employers have paid above the rate to attract or hold labour, and that an agreement has been signed to allow systems of payment by results.

undoubtedly such an exceptional case. But in our proposals we expressly include financial provisions to cover the miners' minimum wage. If the complicated wage system of the industry should ever be rationalized so as to provide for standard wages, it would cover them also. And in any other nationalized industry with similar difficulties we should argue for similar provision.

Finally, we do not wish to exaggerate the importance of our proposals or the magnitude of the effects they are likely to have. Improvements in organization will not produce perfect industries, still less a perfect world. No change in the organization of industry will prevent some consumers feeling that prices are high and the quality of product and service is not quite what it should be; nor prevent many producers feeling that costs are pressing and only superhuman skill and ingenuity could balance accounts at current prices. No change in organization will prevent some workers resenting, as harsh impositions, instructions which seem to managers just and necessary, or prevent some managers feeling that claims, which seem only just and right to the workers who put them forward, are preposterously far-fetched. Under any organization there will be disputes and, on occasion, strikes so long as the right to strike is not forcibly suppressed.

Improved organization cannot spirit these difficulties away, nor can it provide corrective glasses to make different individuals, with very different outlooks, take the same view of industrial events. What it can do, however, is to lessen the likelihood of disputes and crises, and to make more easy the handling of them when they do arise. In smaller organizations there would still be differences of outlook and opinion, but understanding and sympathy would be attained more easily than they are in the nationalized undertakings as they exist to-day.

Having made our disclaimers, we now turn to the details of our proposals.

2. Coal

We have already made it sufficiently clear that we would not have chosen the forms established by the Coal Industry Nationalization Act and the National Coal Board which it established. If it were possible to return to 1946, we would suggest, with the facile wisdom of hind-sight, that the Act should have vested the assets of the industry in a number of district boards, appointed by the Minister. To provide more easily manageable units, some of the smaller districts would have been amalgamated and one or two of the larger districts divided. The few large companies might have been retained as going concerns side by side with the new district boards. The area of each of the district boards and companies would have included a large number of pits (about forty on the average). The duties of the district boards would have been to assume financial control of the colliery undertakings, to prepare development plans and supervise development work, and to provide technical and common services. They would have undertaken the reorganization of collieries by grouping small adjacent pits under a common manager, by closing unremunerative pits and working coal-faces from another shaft, and by the other means already employed under the Coal Board. The authority of the boards would have been limited to these tasks, and in other respects the colliery manager would have retained full responsibility.

The Act would have granted general powers to the Minister, who would be responsible for seeing that the plans, output, and prices of the industry squared up to national needs, if need be by giving directions to one, several, or all of the boards, and perhaps for joining with the boards to provide certain services, such as a 'staff' college or a co-operative research centre. The Act would also have set up a Coal Commission of, say, five or six persons appointed by the Minister, as an expert body and, as far as is humanly possible, an independent body, that is, not allied with any one particular section of the industry. Its duties would have been to advise the Minister on the exercise of his powers, to give technical guidance, where necessary, to the boards, to issue annual reports,[1] and to act as a quasi-judicial body to conciliate disputes between the boards, particularly to compose differences concerning the Coal Charges Account or whatever scheme took its place. The district boards would have had to come together in an association to deal with the unions and probably to deal with the Minister.

Post-mortem examinations have their uses, but there is nothing to be gained by pretending that the Coal Industry Nationalization Act was not passed in 1946 and that the structure of national board, divisional boards, areas, and sub-areas established under the

[1] It is noticeable that the annual reports of the Electricity Commissioners were far less defensive, and in many ways more informative, than the longer reports of the B.E.A.

Act has not had a great effect on the industry. The important question is not what we would like to have seen done in 1946, but how would we propose to change the organization now. Our suggestion is that there is no need for over-all managerial bodies at national or divisional headquarters, but that any reorganization must take into account that the areas have become the main centres for the planning of production and development, and for the provision of technical services. The areas must remain, but it may be that there are too many areas to discharge effectively the tasks we have just mentioned. If their number was reduced to something like half by amalgamating areas, the difficulty of finding enough engineers to provide a first-class team in each area would be greatly reduced, and boundaries might be drawn which would coincide more often with the traditional boundaries of the mining 'districts.' On the other hand, if the new areas were made much larger than the present areas, they might become too big to be effectively controlled by the new area boards even though their responsibilities were limited as we suggest. This question must be left open.[1] Finally, the powers of the Minister should remain, and a Coal Commission should be established.

We may be asked, 'Who would own the industry if this scheme was followed?' A change of ownership is the essence of nationalization. But it is not easy to define the nature of the change. Private ownership ceases, but who becomes the 'owner'? For that matter, who owns the Post Office or Royal Ordnance factories? We may say with pride, 'The Nation,' or with greater

[1] The Coal Board appears to regard the correct size for the areas which it has established as an open question. See p. 63.

regard for legal technicalities, 'The Crown'; but by posing the question we show that few people seriously bother themselves with it. What matters is not 'who is the owner?' but 'how and where are decisions taken?' In the industries with which this essay is concerned, property has been vested in the boards, and this device is as good as another. Are the boards, however, owners in the same way as were the limited companies from which they took over? Or does the Minister, or Parliament, or the nation, now become the owner? And, indeed, does it matter?

Clearly, then, the disposition of property can be settled by consideration of convenience, once it is established that the industry is nationalized, that it is taken out of private hands. Thereafter the important question is the location of powers and not of ownership. So in our proposed reorganization of the mining industry it might be best to make of our new areas public corporations, with their own boards appointed by the Minister, and to vest property in them. A case might be made for vesting in the Coal Commission, and this might work equally well if the Commission could combine the functions of *holding* the property with *advising* on its use. Property might vest in the Crown, but this might seem to give the Minister concerned, and the Treasury, complete responsibility for the industry from top to bottom, as in a government department, and unless this unfortunate consequence could be avoided, it would be better to vest in an 'independent' body.

The observant reader will say of our suggestion for placing the main responsibility for reorganization and development upon area boards: 'This is only the

Lancaster plan rehashed,' and this criticism is so near the mark that we must quote Colonel Lancaster's pamphlet[1] at length:

'In place of the present forty-nine subordinate Areas, there would be set up about half that number of production units which would be largely independent. The Areas which would be represented by those units would bear a direct relation to the producing districts of pre-nationalization days: some districts would be divided into more than one Area, and in other cases small districts would be combined into one Area. There is merit in retaining, wherever useful, some continuity with the experience of the past. These twenty or so Areas, designated not as at present by numbers, but by names familiar in the coal world, would be sufficiently distinct in character and independent in action to command the personal loyalties of those engaged in the industry. The new Areas would in most cases represent a considerably larger task in terms of management than the present Areas. There is, however, more likelihood of finding in the industry to-day twenty to twenty-five men capable of dealing with a larger job of production than of finding forty-nine men of adequate calibre for the smaller job.'

Colonel Lancaster goes on to say that each of the new areas would have its own board and that the chairmen of these boards would be the managing directors. 'Boards of management would free the area general manager from much of the burden of responsibility. Subject to the authority and guidance of their

[1] *The Organization of the Coal Board.* Col. C. G. Lancaster, M.P. Conservative Political Centre, 1948.

Area Chairman, and assisted by a technical staff (or two technical staffs in some of the larger Areas in the Midlands), they would have executive control in matters of coal production and the physical development of their properties.'

Is not our proposal, then, a mere plagiarism? In our view it is not. Colonel Lancaster has chosen for his scheme of reorganization the same boundaries as we would choose for ours, but he would place within those boundaries an organization very different from the one we have outlined. He has seen the difficulties of a Coal Board trying to exert over-all control over divisions, and of divisions trying to exercise over-all control over areas, and advocates the radical solution of setting up 'largely independent' area boards: *within* his areas, as far as we can see, he wants an authority even more powerful than at present, concentrated on a managing director, and an area manager with 'executive control' over production and development. To us this seems almost as unfortunate as the system which it would replace. He would replace one Coal Board which tries to take a whole industry into its grasp by twenty-five boards which would attempt to encompass the whole of the operations of twenty-five large coal-producing areas. We want areas of the same size to be groupings of collieries for the performance of certain functions only, particularly financial control, development planning, and the provision of technical services. We suggest an area board as a useful body to *exercise these functions*, and not to control the collieries in every detail. We look upon these boards rather as holding companies, certainly not as unified commands, with colliery managers, agents, and sub-area managers as the subordinates of an all-powerful managing director and an area manager with full executive control. Another difference between our suggestions and those of Colonel Lancaster is over the Coal Board itself. He is apparently content to leave it in existence, with its present responsibilities. As we have already explained, our view is that so long as there is such a board with general responsibility for the industry, it will be forced to take power into its own hands, however much it may wish to decentralize.

It may be that Colonel Lancaster's error—for such we believe it to be—arises from paying too much regard to the structure of the industry before nationalization. Under private ownership the only means of progress was the extension of ownership by purchase and amalgamation so that larger units could be produced. The drive was usually provided by a man of unusual ability and energy, and organization was built around him. Once the industry is nationalized there is no need to use the same method. Ownership and authority need not run together, and services can be provided where they are needed; there is no need to shape organization to suit a struggle for ownership and power, since that battle has now been fought and won. If Colonel Lancaster is at fault, he did no more than follow the Reid Report, which proposed that 'the conflicting interests of the individual colliery companies are merged together into one compact and unified command of manageable size, with full responsibility, financial and otherwise, for the development of the Area.' Their proposal arose from the difficulties of development and of providing satisfactory services with separate and scattered ownership and arbitrary boundaries between collieries. Once nationalization has disposed of companies and boundaries, however, is there the same need for a 'compact and unified command'? Is it not possible to think rather in terms of the exercise of functions over wider or narrower areas?

Here we must take issue with those who rely on the 'span of control' argument, and choose to quote from amongst our antagonists Sir Henry Self, Deputy Chairman of the B.E.A. He has written:[1]

'We must try to see this industry rather like a big atom. The atom, as you know, has a nucleus, and round the nucleus are a number of shells, which in effect are groups of electrons, maintained by mutual inter-action in their orbits and their respective shells. For example, you have the nucleus and three typical shells called K.L.M. In the industry we have the Central Authority as the nucleus. On the distribution side, we have the 14 Area Boards forming the first shell round the nucleus. To each of these 14 Area Boards there are on the average, say, five Sub-Areas. So the next shell consists of 70 Sub-Areas. The outer shell represents the Districts, and here we have some 500 or 600 District Officers. So we have a nucleus of one, a K shell of 14, an L shell of 70, and an M shell of 500.'

Having constructed a similar 'atom' for generation, Sir Henry goes on:

'It has been argued . . . that we could dispense with the L shell, that is Sub-Areas and Group Headquarters.

[1] Paper on 'Administration and Finance' given to the B.E.A. Summer School at Magdalen College, Oxford, July, 1949.

Why, the critic says, could not the 500 districts and 300 stations work directly to the Area Boards and Divisions respectively? Indeed, the argument might well be enlarged and the question asked—why not eliminate Area Boards and Divisions, why not just have two sides of the sandwich? The answer is simply that headquarters would get jammed up with references and no one would receive an answer without serious delay. We would have 500 undertakings functioning in effect on their own. We have the L shell, because there we can focus the detailed work.'

If the analogy of the atom and its nucleus—which can be as easily applied to coal as to electricity—is a valid analogy, Sir Henry's conclusion is inescapable. If the Coal Board and the B.E.A. are nuclei, they must have a series of shells; they must have regard to the number of subordinates that one man can easily control. Even so, as we have argued earlier, the controller will never be satisfied, for although the nucleus can control the inner shell, its aim is to control the outer shell, and how can the controller ever be sure that the force he exercises over the inner shell is equalled by the force that exerts over the next, and so on?

Our case is that nationalization was necessary to allow certain functions to be exercised over a wider area; to provide these functions groups must be formed and area or regional or national offices established; these offices may, in certain instances, be run by boards, in others by commissioners, in yet others by federal bodies; but there is no need for the offices to become 'headquarters' exercising over-all managerial control from above. Some organizations—for instance, an army or the Foreign Office—must adopt the atomic structure, must have a nucleus with its shells. But the structure has its peculiar strains and stresses, which are multiplied the larger the organization and the more diverse its functions. Since it is not necessary in most of the organizations with which we are here concerned, it should be shunned. Looser forms of organization exist—for instance, the holding company or the employers' federation—and those who administer nationalized industries can learn more from them than from the structure of the atom. The new area boards and the Minister will be given certain limited responsibilities, and in order to discharge them they will have to supervise certain aspects of the industry's work. To provide the information needed to make supervision effective, they will have to rely on the financial and statistical checks which are already being used under the Coal Board. One of the most important tasks of the new area boards and of the commission will be to improve these statistics and extend their use. So long as the new authorities are not required to take general responsibility or to perform tasks which require them to try to acquaint themselves with the details of each colliery's operations, information of this kind will enable them to carry out their duties.

There remain two points on which we wish to touch. We have already stated, and we repeat, that some kind of Coal Charges Account will remain necessary for a long time to come in order to subsidize the wages of the less profitable areas. Subsidies are always troublesome and may easily cover up inefficiency, and the wartime Coal Charges Account was no exception.[1] However, we think its reintroduction would be a small price to pay for an otherwise satisfactory organization in the industry, and we would suggest that it would work much more easily as between twenty-five or thirty financially integrated areas than as between the District Executive Boards set up under the Coal Mines Act of 1930 to operate the district selling schemes; that the particularly hard-hit colliery would now be a matter internal to the area, and not, as under the wartime scheme, a problem for those who manage the account; and, thirdly, that the supervision of the Coal Commission should both aid smooth working and be a powerful check on the misuse of subsidies.

We have so far failed to mention the sale of coal. Is this to become one of the responsibilities of the new areas? We mentioned earlier[2] that there was a case, within the present structure of national and divisional boards, for the transfer of sales from the geographical divisions to an additional *functional* organization which would be responsible for marketing in coal-producing areas and 'white' areas at home and abroad. We think the arguments for this proposal would continue to hold good even if our suggestions for reorganization were carried out. There should be a separate organization, still called, perhaps, the Coal Board, which would purchase coal from the area boards and sell to industrial and domestic consumers. The powers of the Minister and of the Coal Commission would extend over this board as over the area boards, and the Coal Commission would have the responsibility of conciliating

[1] For further information on the Coal Charges Account see *Coal*, W.H.B. Court, H.M.S.O., 1951, Chapter 18.

[2] See p. 61.

any disputes concerning prices between the Coal Board and the area boards. It would be the best body for that purpose, and the settlement of coal prices would, of course, determine the operation of the Coal Charges Account.

3. Electricity

Having expressed our views on the reorganization of the coal industry at some length, it will be possible to deal more briefly with electricity and gas.

It has already been made fairly clear that we regard as regrettable the winding up of the Electricity Commissioners and the replacement of the C.E.B. by the B.E.A. The Act of 1947 might have left those two bodies much as they were, and set up area boards without any direct responsibility to the authority controlling transmission. The Electricity Commissioners could have been accorded much the same duties in relation to the area boards as they already had in relation to the C.E.B. The Minister had no general powers over the C.E.B. and the Act, in granting him powers of direction over the area boards, would have extended those powers also over the C.E.B.

It would be relatively easy to move back to this position. The Commission would have to be re-established, and the authority of the B.E.A. greatly curtailed. The power stations should be transferred to the area boards, although the B.E.A. would retain the same operating control over generation as was used so effectively by the C.E.B.

Several problems would remain to be settled. The dispersion of authority would reintroduce the sale of power from power station to the grid and from the grid to the distributing authority, which might or might not be the authority which owned the power station. Because of the uneven distribution of coal resources and power stations, and because of the difficulty in attributing supply from a particular (say, a high-cost) station to one rather than another of the distributors drawing supplies from the grid, charges would have to be fixed on a basis which would at best be arbitrary. (Although the method of fixing charges certainly need not be more arbitrary than the B.E.A.'s present arrangements with the area boards.) We would hold the view, as over the Coal Charges Account, that this difficulty would be greatly reduced in dealing with fourteen area boards rather than 500 separate undertakings; and that although the problem is not thereby entirely solved, some continuing difficulty in settling charges is a small price to pay for a redistribution of functions which will allow the administrative problems of the industry to be reduced to a manageable size. The Commissioners, as before, could act as an 'independent' (but expert) body for settling disputes over charges.

The location of new power stations is becoming an increasingly difficult problem, and this, together with the determination of quality of design and standardization of equipment, would have to be centrally controlled. Here the Commissioners could continue the work which they performed so well up to 1948.

The limitation of the responsibility of the area boards to 'superior' authority would enable them to relax their grip on the districts which compose them. As with our proposed area coal boards, we would suggest that their task would become much more that of a holding company providing technical services, financial integration, and controlling development. The need for sub-area offices to act as over-all managerial bodies would thus be ended. It might still be desirable to provide some *services* on a sub-area basis; perhaps, as one area board has suggested,[1] different groupings should be arranged for different services, but this would then become a matter of convenience to the board concerned.

The area boards are very large compared with almost all the undertakings which they absorbed. It may well be that it would have been better to establish something like twice the number that now exist. It is doubtful, however, whether, now that the fourteen boards have grown some roots, the disturbance of such a change would be worth while.

There would be need for but little change in the powers and status of the North of Scotland Board. Internally, also, its organization would not require great modification. Perhaps because it is so remote from London, and deals with a vast area and a very scattered population, perhaps also because the bonds tying it to the centralizing B.E.A. are less tight than those of the area boards, its internal organization comes much closer to the pattern we have in mind than do theirs.

The Coal Board has no stock of its own, but borrows from the Treasury which issues stock to cover the loan. This arrangement might continue as well for twenty-five area coal boards as for the National Board; but what would happen to electricity stock? Should it be

[1] See p. 76.

issued by the Commission, the various boards, or the Treasury? We would suggest that there is no principle involved. In private industry, as was noted by all the reports summarized in Chapter I, the larger the concern, the cheaper the raising of capital; but in nationalized industry it is the Treasury guarantee which reduces capital charges. Development must be supervised, but the powers of the Commissioners, and of the Minister and the Cabinet, ensure that the allocation of resources for development will be closely controlled. In these circumstances there appears to be very little reason for not allowing each board to issue its own stock, subject to the powers of the Commissioners and the Minister.

4. Gas

The Area Gas Boards and the Gas Council resemble more closely than any other nationalized industry the general scheme of organization we have in mind. Nevertheless, a few points concerning its organization must be discussed.

Most area boards are large compared with the size of undertakings before nationalization. Smaller area boards might well have provided all the integration and services required. As with area electricity boards, however, we would prefer to leave open the question whether the disturbance of splitting up organizations which have begun to establish their roots would be worth while.

For other nationalized industries we have suggested a national commission to advise boards and the Minister, to deal with disputes within the industry, and to publish reports. Would it be worth while taking away from the Gas Council those functions which are not part of the work of an employers' association, and handing them over to a Gas Commission? (The issue of stock, as we have argued above, could be delegated to the area boards.) The case is not so powerful as in either the coal industry or the electricity industry, but although it may be a counsel of perfection and the right course might be to leave well alone, we feel that the balance of advantage would lie with the change. A Gas Commission would be a more valuable safeguard of the public interest, and could provide better information and advice to the Minister and to Parliament than the Gas Council could ever be expected to do; for the Gas Council must give prior attention to the interests of the area boards which it represents.

Despite the absence of any centralizing influence so powerful as the B.E.A., most of the area gas boards have probably gone too far in trying to make of themselves over-all managerial bodies and in developing divisional organization as a means of establishing their grip over gas works and distribution. The example of the Wales Gas Board, and perhaps also the Eastern Board, could serve as a model to some of its fellows.

There is, however, nothing to be gained by pretence that a common pattern would suit all areas. Areas which include one of the country's vast urban conglomerations cannot copy the organization of the mainly rural areas; and the North Thames Gas Board must operate as a single integrated undertaking. If its organization is on too large a scale—or, for that matter, if London Transport is too big—the fault lies not with those who planned the organization, but with the size of London itself.

5. The Co-ordination of Fuel and Power

So far our main thesis has been that if a higher authority is made generally responsible for the conduct of an industry it must centralize functions which would be better left to individual undertakings or to area authorities. In the co-ordination of fuel and power we come across a problem which is almost the exact reverse of this; for here we have a higher authority—the Minister—who will not use the powers granted to him to discharge a function which he must perform if it is to be performed at all.

There can be little question that there is a job to be done. A decision on the development of electricity supply at pit-head stations from low quality fuels ought not to be left to the interested parties. If the area gas boards complain that their interests are neglected in the determination of prices for different qualities of coal, the Minister must intervene to settle the dispute.

Co-ordination by the Minister would be rendered more easy if the changes we have suggested were made. He would not then have to deal with national managerial boards anxious for their authority and prestige. He would have the advantage of advice from relatively independent and expert commissions who should be able to see the matters in dispute in their right perspective. He would still, however, need the courage to make use of his powers.

The remedy which has recently been tried—the device of the super-Minister to co-ordinate all the nationalized industries—appears to be designed to confuse responsibilities more than before. If the fuel and power industries alone are concerned, the Minister of Fuel and Power has authority; if other industries are concerned, the Cabinet or the Prime Minister can intervene as they could in other matters in which more than one Ministry is concerned. The will to use existing powers will not be strengthened by setting up an imposing new authority to whom the 'buck' may be passed.

If there is a genuine need for further information before action is taken, surely the right course is to appoint a committee to investigate a specific problem and report; not to establish a new permanent authority, whether it is a super-Minister, a super-commission, or a super-board.

6. The Transport Commission

Fuel and power co-ordination is a matter of importance secondary to the internal reorganization of the three industries concerned, or, at least, it requires a limited number of major decisions rather than constant attention; for this reason it may properly be left to the Minister. Transport co-ordination is perhaps the central problem of transport, and at least as intricate a problem as the internal reorganization of the services concerned. Co-ordination of transport requires continuous attention and forward planning. This was recognized by the authors of the Transport Act, and they were probably right in establishing a separate Transport Commission whose main concern was to be co-ordination.

If the establishment of the Commission was justified, its continued existence is also justified. The problem of co-ordination is so complex that it would be foolish to say, after only four years, that co-ordination has failed; but it is abundantly clear that it has not yet succeeded, and, therefore, that the Commission's task is as vital now as on vesting day.

The Transport Act gave general authority to the Commission, and provided that schemes of delegation might be drawn up to grant some of the Commission's functions to the Executives, who were to act as agents of the Commission. For reasons already explained we would prefer a strict limitation of the duties of the Commission to co-ordination. In fact, the Commission has tended to use its authority in matters which could best be left to the separate services; in some instances it has been forced to do so because of the width of its responsibilities.

A limitation of this kind would not, however, make of the Transport Commission a body parallel to the commissions which we have proposed for coal, electricity, and gas. For one thing, the Transport Act vested inland transport undertakings in the Commission. But perhaps this is not a major difference between the two types of commission. We have already expressed the opinion that once property is nationalized, it is not the formal ownership but the distribution of authority which counts. There is, then, no weighty reason for dispossessing the Transport Commission, and the convenience of leaving the matter where it stands is emphasized by the method used by the Commission to exercise its powers over such undertakings as Thomas Cook's and the road passenger concerns of which it is the sole owner or part owner. In road passenger transport the Commission acts as a holding company with reserve powers, and entrusts the integration of services and the supervision of operations to the Tillings and Scottish Group Organizations. We should not like to see this arrangement disturbed.

A more important difference between the proposed commissions for the fuel and power industries and the Transport Commission is this: the former commissions were to be mainly advisory, the latter will retain important, even if limited, executive powers for co-ordination. It should, however, be possible for the Commission to combine this responsibility with the duty of advising the Minister in the exercise of his powers over the separate services, duties which he must retain in the interests of national planning. The Commission will not be as 'independent' as the Electricity Commissioners, and it will not be able to take an impartial attitude on occasions when the Minister wishes to use his powers in matters of co-ordination; but to set up one commission to co-ordinate and another commission to advise the Minister on co-ordination would seem to be a clumsy multiplication of authorities.

. . . . .

Concerning four of the Executives we have little to add to what we have already written. Restaurant-car and refreshment-room services might with advantage return to the railways, although the hotels might remain as a separate undertaking.[1] There do not appear to be strong grounds for disturbing the Docks and Inland

[1] See p. 95.

Waterways Executive; it would certainly be fanciful to suppose that a reorganization would turn it into a highly profitable concern.[1] The organization of London Transport is suited to the size and shape of Greater London.[2] And in its method of control of its provincial road passenger services the Transport Commission has come close to the form of administration which we should like to see in general use in the nationalized industries.[3]

We cannot, however, dismiss the railways and road haulage so briefly as this. They must be discussed separately and in greater detail.

7. The Railway Executive

In the nationalized railways the functional organization of the L.M.S. Railway has become the model and has been extended to cover all the four companies taken over. They have been converted into six regions, each of which has a regional officer with strictly limited authority,[4] so that the departmental officers at the region work to the chief officers of the Executive itself. We wish to question the assumptions on which this organization is based, and we shall begin by questioning the assumption that the tasks of the various departments are so different that each must have a different geographical area for its districts, and consequently, each departmental district officer must be independent of his colleagues in other departments.

Before nationalization the Mechanical Engineering Departments of the four companies dealt with the design, production, and maintenance of rolling-stock.

[1] See p. 99. [2] See p. 101. [3] See p. 96. [4] See p. 112.

The explanation for the undertaking of production by the companies is historical. Accordingly we can leave design and production aside. The workers of the Mechanical Engineering Department are concentrated in a few engineering works, which are run, and must be run, as a service for the system as a whole, and cannot be brought into any district organization. The Police Department is now run as a central service by the Transport Commission, and the six police areas have been chosen to fit in as far as possible with civil police boundaries. The departments with a district organization are: Operating, Commercial, Motive Power, Civil Engineering, Signals and Telecommunications, Estates and Rating, and Marine. Of these seven we can quickly dispose of the last two. The relatively few marine districts are geographically separate from the rest of the system, and have also a distinct function. Estates and rating is a business quite separate from railway operating matters, and can be managed, like mechanical engineering or police, as a common service.

There remain five types of district, whose work must be closely related. Amongst them Motive Power has only recently been organized as a separate department. There could therefore be no great difficulty about its reintegration if the other departments could be brought together in one unit.

Amongst the remaining departments, Operating and Commercial are by far the largest. If we can offer good reason for their amalgamation, the remainder of our task should not be too difficult. A point in our favour is that even now they are not everywhere separated. It is true that the Southern Region is exceptional in the low volume of freight it is called on to handle, but even so, it is worthy of note that it has continued the six *Traffic* Districts of the old Southern Railway. Again, the Scottish Region has combined the work of its Commercial and Operating Departments in four of its districts.

The main argument for separation is that the considerations for the delimitation of an Operating District are the length of line and the density of flow, whereas the chief criterion for a Commercial District is the density of population and of industry. But if the Commercial District is centred on one area of dense population such as Manchester or Birmingham, surely each extension of its radius to approximate to the radius of the Operations District would be likely to take in a smaller increment in population. Ten miles around the centre of Birmingham will give a Commercial District a great deal of work; if it can cope with that, is an extension of its responsibility to twenty or thirty miles around Birmingham going to break its back? An outsider can do no more than ask this question, point to the Traffic Districts of the Southern and Scottish Regions, and point to the immense advantages of a unified undertaking of comprehensible size.

If all Commercial, Operating, and Motive Power Districts could be amalgamated into Traffic Districts, there could not be any major objection to bringing Civil Engineering under the same common district management. Signalling and Telecommunications might present some technical difficulty over the telephone system, but this obstacle ought not to be insurmountable. Despite the trunk system which it operates, the Post Office is able to divide up its telephone work into about fifty areas under area managers who have considerable authority.

We hold the view, then, that unless there is some obstacle to unification which the railway experts have not yet made plain, it would be possible to map out a number of districts which could bring together in a single headquarters and under a single district manager all those aspects of railway work which are not obviously central services. The district manager would be assisted by appropriate specialists, but their responsibility would be to him and not to regional specialists.

The size of these new districts might be much the same as the size of the present Operating Districts, to give about fifty districts for the whole country; or it might be found more convenient to have rather fewer and therefore larger districts. For instance, the old Control Divisions of the L.M.S. Railway, which for certain purposes were interposed between the Operating Districts and the company's headquarters, might provide a more suitable area. There were three of these divisions south of the Scottish border.

A change of this kind should have important consequences for industrial relations. The bad effects on industrial relations of the present structure of the Railway Executive have been described in an interesting Fabian pamphlet.[1] The thesis of this pamphlet has been denied by no one. The only objections have been that it is impossible to alter the present structure of the Executive.

A critic might say that the reorganization which we propose would make of the new districts undertakings

[1] *British Railways—The Human Problem*, by Frank Pickstock, Fabian Research Series, 142, 1950.

still too large to make sense to the ordinary worker, too large to make a serious difference to industrial relations. It is true that the new districts would be big. Supposing there were to be thirty of them, they would have on the average a staff of about twenty thousand workers. The three divisions of the old L.N.E.R., however, were considerably larger than this, and yet the Fabian pamphlet mentioned above is able to say: 'There is little doubt that there was less bureaucracy and more human touch in the management of the L.N.E.R. than in that of the highly centralized L.M.S.' If this is true, unified *districts* should offer even greater advantages.

To put our proposal in other words, we wish to undo a great deal of the work of the 1921 Act. The framers of that Act were right in thinking that certain functions in the industry ought to be centralized. Because they thought in terms of private amalgamation and because they were convinced of the advantages of bigness, they centralized those functions by pushing the many existing undertakings into a small number of vast concerns. No doubt they also thought that by this means they could avoid a bitter struggle over each extension of central authority. But it would have been possible to arrange a grouping of functions without the creation of the four mammoth companies.

There is a popular misconception that because the railways of this country form one system they must be run by a single management. If we can cast our minds back to the period before the 1921 Act, however, we must admit that it is possible for many separate railway undertakings to exist, and at the same time for the close-knit railway system of this country to operate as one system for the carriage of goods and passengers. If that was possible with many separately-owned companies, surely it should be all the more possible with a number of separate district organizations within one nationally-owned railway system. The 1914–18 war, and indeed also the second world war, showed the advantages of common action, standardization and central direction in some matters, but under nationalization it is not difficult to obtain common action, or to give central direction where it is needed, without the establishment of an all-powerful Railway Executive.

It is true that the bulk of railway traffic was local traffic before 1921, but this is still the case. In 1950 the average distance per passenger journey for all categories of ticket was just over twenty miles, and for ordinary tickets (that is, excluding season tickets, workmen's tickets, and so on) just under thirty miles. The average length of haul for freight was longer, but still just under seventy-five miles (for all classes of freight).

If we may suppose, for the moment, that our case is established that, apart from certain separate central services, railway operations should be brought together into unified districts under a single management, what would be the consequences for the regional organizations and for the Railway Executive itself? Should they remain to provide the central services we have mentioned; should they be replaced by other bodies; or should they be disbanded?

Regional and national organization will certainly be required for part of the work of the railways. There will be need for co-ordination in research and in the design and production of rolling-stock. Common action will have to be taken in operating methods and in train control. Accounting and finance must be a central service. The railway unions will insist on the maintenance of national collective bargaining for the whole railway staff. Indeed, one of the complaints of the unions is that nationalization has not been followed, as they expected it would be, by an extension of the standard grading system, already accepted by the companies, to a standard specification of jobs for each grade to prevent different rates being paid for the same work in different regions. At present each region may choose which jobs go within a given grade, although the rate to be paid to that grade is agreed nationally. The local application of national agreements has traditionally been a matter for sectional councils for the various grades of workers. These councils used to cover the areas of each company, and are now regional bodies. The unions would probably also wish them to retain their present functions. In addition, common action would be necessary in dealings with the Commission and the Minister. The exact allocation of those tasks between national and regional headquarters would require investigation and expert advice.[1]

If there are these functions which require regional and national organization, would it not be best to entrust them to the existing bodies rather than to throw the whole system into confusion by extending

[1] For a railway officer's view on the proper allocation of functions between the regions and national headquarters, and for an interesting expression of opinion on railway organization in general, see a letter of G. L. Nicholson to the editor of the *Railway Gazette*, printed in the issue of 23rd May, 1952, under the title of 'The White Paper and British Railways.'

radical reorganization beyond the districts? Whatever weight this consideration may have we feel to be overborne by another. Instead of acting as an over-all management, or as the regional feelers of such a management, national and regional headquarters should become group organizations whose main purpose is to provide services required by the districts. Because of their present functions and their long traditions of centralized control, we do not believe that the present regional or national headquarters could be moulded into this new pattern. If the same personnel and outward forms remained, they would naturally try to re-establish their over-all authority, and those who work in the local and district units might well feel that once again what purported to be a great change had left everything much as it always was. For these reasons we submit that it would be advisable to replace the Railway Executive and the regional headquarters by new devices of organization.

What do we propose to put in their place? To this question we do not wish to give a detailed reply. So long as the new organizations are designed to carry out those functions which must be performed over a wider area than the district, and to supply to the districts those services which they cannot conveniently and economically supply within their own boundaries, and to do no more than this, they will satisfy our conditions. It might be best to form regional group organizations of the district managers, who would meet periodically to review the work of the region. Nationally an organization akin to the Tillings or Scottish Group Management Boards for road passenger transport might be responsible to the Commission for the supply of central services to the railway regions and districts, and for supervision of the working of the railway system on the Commission's behalf. These are, however, no more than suggestions of the kind of organization that is required. A number of different proposals might be made to give an organization which would suit our purposes as well, or perhaps better.

The district and regional organizations of the railways could not have exactly the same status as area coal, electricity, or gas boards, unless the Railway Clearing House were re-established to allow their accounts to be separated. Although the jibe may be true that the Railway Executive has got rid of the Clearing House by setting up even more committees than the Clearing House ever knew, the resurrection of the Clearing House would not be a useful move. If it were to be brought back as part of the suggested scheme of reorganization, its task in separating out the accounts of districts, regions, and a central office supplying central services would be a far more complicated task than when it served the four companies. It is important that each section of the system should know how it is going, how its operations compare with those of other sections, but sampling checks and statistical analyses can well provide for this.

The advantages of centralized accounting and financial control must be admitted, but they do not constitute good grounds, any more than do the advantages of centralized workshop services or standard designs and operating methods, for the centralization of the whole of railway organization.

8. The Road Haulage Executive

The outstanding problem of road haulage organization is not the departmentalization of the railways, but the number of tiers in the hierarchic structure of the Executive—division, district, group, and depot. Nevertheless, we suggest the remedy should be similar to that which we have just proposed for railway organization. The Executive's services, like those of the railways, constitute a national system which for technical reasons (to provide balanced running and directional services[1]) requires that some functions are performed over a wide area. But there is no need for national or regional over-all management to provide this.

Concentration of depots is already reducing the number of depots to a group. It might be possible to carry this process further by cutting out the group altogether, and making the district the unit of over-all management. Since the Executive has about 80,000 employees and thirty districts, a change of this kind should provide units of a workable size. It would also assist the co-ordination of road and rail. If co-ordination is to be more than a central pooling of receipts, road and rail organization must be interlinked at operational level. Therefore, there should be a continuing effort to draw common boundaries for road haulage and railway districts, and the functions and authority of the district managers in the two sections of the industry should be as nearly as possible the same.

[1] These services are provided by depots or groups which take responsibility for all traffic proceeding in a given direction from their own districts.

The experiment in East Anglia[1] is most emphatically a move in the right direction. The appointment of a manager responsible to both railways and road services is not essential to the scheme, and should probably not be imitated elsewhere. The other shortcomings of the experiment are that it does not go far enough, and it covers only a small area. Since it is the right direction, it should be followed at more than a snail's pace.

If road haulage districts are developed in this way, divisional organization (if it is still needed at all) should provide centres for common action over those functions and services which should be performed over an area wider than the district. Divisions should cease to be over-all commands, and it might be best to emphasize their character as service centres by using the Wales Gas Board device of group organization. If this were done, divisional committees of district managers would be set up to take charge of divisional services.

The function of the Road Haulage Executive has so far been very different from that of the Railway Executive. The latter has tried to *run* the railways; the first duty of the Road Haulage Executive has been to build up a national road haulage organization. Because of the enormous complexity of this task it had to be carried out by a central authoritative body such as the Executive. The job is not yet finished. The rapid intake of undertakings has ceased, but there has not yet been time to complete the job of welding them together. Until it is finished, there is need for the Executive, and thereafter, so long as it avoids the example of the Railway Executive, the Road Haulage Executive might remain as the best body to provide

[1] See p. 121.

central services and to supervise. Alternatively, it might then be best to replace it with the kind of organization we have already suggested for the railways.

. . . . .

In May, 1952, the Conservative Government published a White Paper[1] entitled 'Transport Policy.' Concerning railway organization it stated simply that 'the present excessive centralization of railways must, however, be reduced by giving greater autonomy to areas which may follow the general pattern of the present regions.' It may be that behind this change of name lies careful thought on the proper distribution of functions between the Executive, the regions, and the districts; or it may be that there is very little behind it. The auction of 'operable units (including a suitable proportion of small units)' of road haulage assets will, however, surely and radically alter the organization of the road haulage industry, and destroy any possibility of road-rail integration of freight transport. The administrative arrangements for this sale will not be easy, but that is a minor matter. The losses expected in the sale are more important. The hostility of the unions, the bad effects of the upheaval on the staff, and the difficulty of arranging compensation for those who will lose their livelihood are even more serious matters. Most important of all, however, is the proposal to meet the losses from the sale and the loss to the railways caused by 'further transfer of traffic from rail to road' by 'a levy on goods vehicles.' To subsidize the railways out of a tax raised on road haulage undertakings is a

[1] Cmd. 8538 of 1952.

clumsy and unpopular device. Since the very suggestion of such a subsidy admits so much of the case for co-ordination, it would perhaps be best, after all, to give co-ordination the few more years that are required to show what it can do.

9. Other Nationalized Industries

We have no proposals to make concerning the two other nationalized industries which have been discussed in the previous chapters—Air Transport and Steel. The two Airways Corporations are relatively small organizations, and the analysis which we have tried to apply to the fuel and power and inland transport industries would not apply directly to them. Besides that, each corporation has been the subject of more than one thorough reorganization during the last few years. Air Transport is a rapidly developing industry, but even so, a major reorganization every three years, or even more frequently, may perhaps be too much of a good thing.

The Iron and Steel Corporation has hardly developed any organization as yet and, if proposals for de-nationalization are embodied in legislation, it may never do so. If the industry remains nationalized there is need for a reallocation of functions between the corporation, the federation, and a Ministry (which has retained powers of the kind that the Ministries of Fuel and Power and of Transport passed over to the boards concerned on vesting day). Whatever the right allocation of central authority, whether the structure of the federation should be modified or not, and whether there is need for a corporation if the Ministry retains direct controls, we are certain that a hierarchic structure of over-all area and regional management bodies would not serve to make the industry either more efficient or happier.

10. Finding the Managers

In the last chapter[1] we admitted that no scheme of reorganization would deserve serious attention unless it could be shown that the men could be found to make it work. We must now face up to this challenge.

Workers in nationalized industries, at least the more militant trade unionists amongst them, are often strongly critical of their managers, senior technicians, and boards. They complain that they are the same old gang, that many of them are unsympathetic to nationalization and to 'the aspirations of the workers,' and they are free with the words 'sabotage' and 'saboteur.' On the other hand, Ministers and the boards themselves say that there was need for continuity of personnel if the industries were to run through the change-over, that training new managers and new technicians takes many years, that the higher staff of the industry is a skilled, competent, and public-spirited body of men, and that talk of sabotage is irresponsible stupidity.

These two views are, to say the least of it, not easily reconciled. If, therefore, we must choose the one or the other, is it not only sensible to take the second view? There are, of course, difficulties in selecting staff. It is unfortunate that some of the indispensable managers and technicians have perhaps rather an old-fashioned view of relationships between manager and man,

[1] See p. 158.

between employer and trade union. It is unfortunate that the cost of compensating managers who drew high salaries before nationalization forces the boards to retain some men whom they would prefer to be without. But, taking all in all, is it not likely that the boards will have found and used the best men available? Are they not developing schemes of promotion and training which will open the highest posts to talent wherever in the industry it is to be found? And is it not foolish romanticism to talk of sabotage in the solid, sensible Britain of 1952?[1]

Our answer to these questions cannot be an unqualified 'yes.' Of course, the board member's case is far more sensible and more easily argued than the case of the militant trade union member. Of course, the latter uses words like sabotage when all he means is 'lack of enthusiasm,' 'unwillingness to see my point of view,' or perhaps 'bureaucratic inefficiency.' And we are all thankful that in Britain we do not use the gallows, or even the prison camp, as the remedy for inefficiency. When all this is admitted, however, there remains some substance in the 'left-wing' case. Besides those who are kept on to earn some part of the money that must be paid to them as compensation, there are some managers in nationalized industry who do not believe it can work and cannot, with the best will in the world, put heart and soul into their work; there are certainly some men who, in the hurried months before

[1] 'I have been accustomed in this Congress to say the things I believe and as far as I can see there was no sign of political bias operating at any stage in the transition processes, and believe me there were many possibilities for that bias to have interfered with the smooth transition.'—LORD CITRINE, in his address to the Trade Union Congress at Brighton, 1950.

and after vesting days, were appointed to jobs they ought never to have held. These, however, are the exceptions. They may serve as ammunition for the trouble-maker, but the industry as a whole cannot be judged by them. It is also true that in time they will be replaced.

In our view, however, a more serious shortcoming does lie behind the charges that are made. Workers did expect great changes from nationalization, some of them no doubt beyond the possibility of realization. Amongst other things they expected a change in their own status and treatment within their industry, and in the event many of them feel bitterly disappointed. To go any considerable distance towards satisfying these hopes there would have had to be a radical change in the attitude and approach of most of the industry's managers towards those under their control. An immediate and large-scale change of this kind was no doubt out of the question; but more could have been done since then, and much could be done now. By what means? We submit that there is a quality of human sympathy, of willingness and ability to understand other men and women, to comprehend their motives and to appreciate their point of view, even when clumsily expressed, which some people possess in high degree, others in moderation, and in which still others are deficient. There is also a quality of leadership, of readiness to take responsibility, and capacity to bring others along in whatever course is finally chosen, to which the same remarks apply. Where they exist, these qualities can be fostered and strengthened. In the past, the not very distant past, industry has generally looked for other qualities than these, especially technical qualifications and skills. The militant trade unionist who assumes that most 'horny-handed workers' are endowed by birth and environment with these qualities of sympathy and leadership, and that no ex-public school boy can possess them, is certainly wrong; but he would be right if he said that not enough attention is yet paid to these qualities, and that some of those who occupy managerial positions because of education or other qualifications, or because of advancement prior to nationalization, possess them not at all.

We would stress once again that specialist advice in personnel management cannot by itself remedy bad management of men. If, however, sufficient weight was given to these qualities by selection boards, and if the disposition of staff between advisory, technical, and managerial posts was determined by such considerations more than it is, the management of men should improve noticeably. Complaints and grievances would be more skilfully handled, joint consultative committees would give more satisfaction because their chairmen would appreciate what could be made of them, workers would know that they could get an answer to their questions and problems, and an answer on which they could rely. We also stress, however, that the selection of managers more capable in this respect could achieve little within an organization designed to frustrate them rather than to give them scope.

It is frequently said that the trade unions are the greatest centralizing force in nationalized industry, and the statement contains more than a grain of truth. The unions themselves are centralized organizations. Their duty is to care for the interests of their members, and if there is a national authority with over-all responsibility, they are only doing their job when they seek to have the unfavourable decisions of subordinate authorities reversed by it. A limitation of the functions of national and regional authorities would reduce the size of the problem; but it may be objected that the unions could never be brought to accept such a limitation. We cannot agree with this proposition. Some trade unionists begin to realize that the more potent the checks on the local manager lest he prove unsatisfactory, the more frequent the complaints that union members and shop stewards 'can get no satisfaction,' that the settlement of complaints and grievances is delayed. Centralization is the trade union's defence against bad management. If able and sympathetic local managers can be found, a redistribution of functions would be a positive benefit to the unions.

The right qualities cannot be created by training, but training can draw them out where they exist. There has already been some development of training for managers in the nationalized industries; it could with profit receive far greater attention.

To suggest methods of discovering and developing talent is, however, to fight only half the battle. For at best the supply of talent is limited. Accordingly, the best use must be made of talent when it is found.

Reorganization on the lines suggested would assist the best use of talent in two ways. First, the nationalized industries would make less lavish demands for talent and for genius. The pre-war public corporations, the B.B.C., the C.E.B., and the L.P.T.B., had a Lord Reith, an Andrew Duncan, and a Lord Ashfield. Genius far greater than theirs would be needed to perform all that is required of the Coal Board or the B.E.A., yet the post-war corporations have hardly produced their equals. *It would be more sensible to construct an organization without national managerial boards than to hope that some day the superman needed to run them may be forthcoming.*

Secondly, each regional or area board would be free to choose its own headquarters organization and to staff this organization as it thought fit. They would not have to abide by a standard establishment. Each board would no doubt require a secretary, an accountant, a lawyer, and one or more engineers, but there would be no need to staff departments up to establishment without regard to the men available. It would be a great advantage that consultancy services could be designed to suit the men available; and if good men could not be found for a particular service, it would not have to be provided. Incompetent consultants can do widespread damage.

One of the most important advantages of these changes would be that more first-rate men would be available for the post of operational manager. Moreover, a reduction in the number of his superiors and the limitation of their authority would enhance the status of the operational manager's job and make it more attractive to first-class men. If this does happen, industrial relations should benefit handsomely.

11. Conclusion

It may now be useful to bring together the main points of our thesis.

Whether it wishes to do so or not, Parliament must

take responsibility for the national economy, and nationalization is one of the instruments to hand for the discharge of this responsibility. By 1945 it was widely accepted that only by means of nationalization could the rapid and thorough reorganization of our basic industries be ensured. Over the last few years, however, nationalization has fallen into disrepute. The reason for this is not anything inherent in nationalization itself, but the type of organization which has been imposed on the industries nationalized since 1945.

It would have been possible to nationalize each undertaking separately and to allow it to continue as an independent concern, with government-appointed directors. This would have prevented the attainment of many of the aims of nationalization; for one of the most pressing arguments for nationalization (except in the case of steel) was the need for many functions to be performed over a much wider area, and for some functions to be performed on a national scale.

The only solution to the problem thus presented was to see that national and regional bodies carried out those tasks which had to be centralized, and left the operational units of the industries concerned as much freedom as possible to carry out their duties within the limits imposed by central decisions. This, however, is just what the nationalizers would claim to have done. The nationalization Acts established national boards, or national and regional boards, and made them responsible for their industries. It was the intention of the legislators that these boards should make their own arrangement for a devolution of such functions as could be better discharged over a narrower area to the undertakings themselves, or to managers or boards responsible for groups of undertakings. This intention was fulfilled. The boards have established divisional, regional, area, sub-area, group, and district managements, according to their taste in titles, and entrusted many matters to them, or through them to the operational managers. What more could have been done?

In our view, an arrangement of this kind must result in over-centralization for two reasons. The first is that once the central bodies have been given over-all responsibility for their industries by Parliament, those with grievances against subordinate authorities will pursue them to the central body or to the Minister, who will raise the matter in question with the central body, so that adequate decentralization becomes impossible. The second reason is that if the central bodies have general responsibility, and cannot judge their subordinates by the test of profitability, they must construct their organizations on what we have called the 'span of control' pattern. To allow each superior officer or board to exercise full control over his subordinates, he must maintain personal contact with them and have personal knowledge of their work. Accordingly, the number of subordinates which can be controlled by a single officer or board is closely limited, and a tall pyramid of organization becomes inevitable.

Something has already been said of the disadvantages of this structure. Here it will serve to repeat that to perform properly the duties of a member of one of the national boards is a task for a superman; that the advantages of standardization and central purchasing of major equipment are outweighed by the disadvantages of standard administrative procedures, without regard to local differences, and of standard establishments, without regard to the men available; that the demand for talent is further inflated by the number of levels of management; and that the local manager is not encouraged to do his best, in particular that it is not made easy for him to foster good industrial relations.

Is there, then, an alternative form of organization which will avoid these difficulties and still give the benefits of nationalization? We think there is. Parliament should decide what functions can be and should be exercised over an area wider than the individual undertaking and place responsibility *for these functions alone* upon appropriate regional and national authorities.

The design of 'appropriate' authorities would require thought and research, but we have tried to show that there are grounds for believing that a redistribution of functions is possible, even on the railways, and that the holding company, the employers' federation, the trade association, and the Electricity Commission provide models for the bodies to perform them which deserve attention, though not slavish imitation. The general outline of our scheme of reorganization may be summarized by saying that regional or area authorities should serve as holding companies to plan and supervise development and to exercise financial control over the operational units; that the Minister, advised by an independent commission, should supervise the work of these authorities and see that they meet the requirements of national planning; and that a federation of regional authorities should negotiate with the unions and meet the Minister.

Reform on these lines should proceed cautiously and slowly. Administrative upheavals will not give good results. Nevertheless, reform should be undertaken, and if carried out it should bring solid benefits. Reorganization would encourage better work from board members and senior officers because the demands made upon them would then be demands which they could meet. Standardization would then be more closely limited to those functions in which standardization is profitable. Local administrative experiments would be encouraged. It would be possible to establish and distribute local and regional managerial and 'staff' posts to suit the number and qualities of the men available, and those appointed to these posts would be less likely to find good work made impossible by bureaucratic restrictions. The public would have more confidence in the reports and supervision of semi-independent, mainly advisory, commissions than they can have in the best of managerial boards. Decisions of major importance to the nation would be taken by the Minister, using his powers openly and responsibly, after consultation with one of these commissions.

A reorganization of this kind would do far more to better industrial relations and to give workers something of the improved status and treatment which they expected from nationalization than the appointment of ex-trade union officials to boards, the elaboration of collective bargaining procedures, or the provision of consultative committees can, of themselves, ever give.

We have made proposals concerning individual industries. They are only illustrations, not blue-prints. They probably require correction and certainly require amplification, but detailed planning must be left to the experts. Organizations and their constitutions, however, are the expression of thoughts and opinions. The purpose of our essay has not been to elaborate complete plans for reorganizing the nationalized industries, but to try to influence thinking about their organization towards the belief which we hold—that the future of nationalization depends on discovering and using means to make national ownership and national planning compatible with small-scale operation.